THE LEADERSHIP CONTRADICTION

Choosing a Path of Love and Kindness

by Traycee Mayer

Ordering Information:
Special discounts are available on quantity purchases by corporations, associations, educational institutions, and others. For details, contact Traycee Mayer above.

Printed in the United States of America

First Edition

ISBN 979-8-88896-435-4

Publisher: Dreamwave Press an Imprint of Superbrand Publishing

DEDICATION

Appreciation in abundance to my son Brandon
whose love continues to give me wings

Gratitude to my rescue cats Ninja and Shadow
who gave me the vision I needed to trust fall

ACKNOWLEDGEMENTS

This book would not gotten off the ground if it was not for the loving support and kind feedback from Jeaneen Sullivan, a consummate professional, great line editor and hilarious travel buddy.

Karen Gunther was my number one cheerleader and gave me what I strive to give to so many others, unconditional love, and encouragement regularly, and she even attended my graduation at the UC Berkeley Coaching Institute!

Finally, Sharon Noot, when your plate was overflowing, you still found time for me to help get me over the hump.

This book is a miracle in itself and so are the gifts of friendship and mutual respect from the 3 unique humans that you are! Thank you all!

PRAISE FOR THE LEADERSHIP CONTRADICTION

Ms. Mayer's book on leadership is the one you've been missing! Filled with raw emotion and vulnerability, **The Leadership Contradiction** *takes you on a journey of deep introspection and discovery that all leaders need to travel to attain their highest level of effectiveness. It reminds us that we have choices and regardless of the outcomes, there are powerful lessons to be learned in every destination. In a world that's moving at the speed of light where capital is king in business,* **The Leadership Contradiction** *is an opportunity to choose a path where love is at the center and the positive impacts are limitless.*

Dawn Graham, PhD, Author of "Switchers: How Smart Professionals Change Careers and Seize Success"

Employees and managers alike are thirsty for better ways to connect, produce and deliver in the marketplace, and **The Leadership Contradiction** *quenches that thirst. It shows that raising the bar on love and kindness can actually elevate productivity, retention, and every other success metric within an organization. What a timely and refreshing read!*

Renessa Boley Layne, Founder, Creating Your Perfect Work and Author - Fast Lane, Wrong Direction: Insider Secrets to Redesign Your Success

Traycee guides you along the path to authentic leadership, embracing your true self and discovering who you are meant to be in this complex and confusing world. **The Leadership Contradiction** *is a gem of a read that will captivate you from beginning to end.*

Marcel Schwantes, Global Speaker, Author, and Renowned Leadership Coach

Today, love others for who they are. See the beauty in the journey.
Hold your head high and be brave. Extend a hand, give back.
Believe in the power of simply being kind.
—Rachel Marie Martin

CONTENTS

FOREWORD

I have been deeply and profoundly inspired by the contents of this book, and even more so by my personal relationship with Traycee Mayer. In "**The Leadership Contradiction**," Traycee takes you on a heartfelt, authentic exploration of the complex and often paradoxical nature of what we are told is effective leadership. In a world where leadership theories abound, Traycee takes a bold step by embracing the idea that leadership can reach its peak effectiveness with a loving and kind approach. She guides readers through the different paths that they often face, illuminating how blocks, mistakes, and chaos can lead to innovation and growth. Traycee reminds us that leadership is not merely a title or a position; it's a choice—a choice to uplift, inspire, and empower those around us. She shares her vulnerable and courageous journey from contradictions to clarity as an inspiring testament to the transformative power of conscious leadership.

In a world that often glorifies ruthless ambition, "**The Leadership Contradiction**" is a refreshing reminder that true leadership is about nurturing the human spirit, fostering growth, and leaving a legacy of impact through a loving and kind approach. It is a call to action—a call to lead with your heart and your unwavering commitment to the betterment of humanity. While some have experienced cynicism and self-interest in the workplace, this book dares to shine a light on the brighter side of leadership—a side that can transform workplaces, communities, the future, and life itself. Traycee's unique insights and ability to reframe leadership challenges as opportunities make this book an indispensable guide for navigating the convoluted landscape of leadership in today's ever-evolving world.

Whether you're a seasoned executive or just starting your leadership journey, this book will undoubtedly enrich your perspective and equip you with the tools to embrace all the different leadership paths you will embark on. As you journey along the illuminating path in "**The Leadership Contradiction**," be prepared to leave feeling challenged to do things better than you've done before and inspired to take responsibility for making a difference in today's world. Traycee offers practical examples that you can immediately implement to make a positive difference in the lives of others. With every turn of the page, you'll uncover valuable insights and strategies to lead with love, kindness, and authenticity.

"**The Leadership Contradiction**" is a must-read for anyone who aspires to become a more effective and dynamic leader who wants to leave a legacy for the greater good. I'm honored to play a small role in helping to bring this hopeful message of love and kindness to leadership. Enjoy this wonderful book and may you always recognize the gifts along your path.

Amy Lynn Durham

CEO, Create Magic At Work ®

Chapter 1:

THE HIKE

Inner Revelations

"This journey served as a reflection and realization of the paths we choose and how we navigate our leadership roles and our lives."
—**Traycee Mayer**

It was a quiet and blissful Christmas morning in 2020, a cool California morning with the sun brightly shining, beckoning me to a local hiking trail that I had traversed on bike and by foot for many years. As I dressed and prepared for the hours-long trek, I noticed my fur babies, Ninja and Shadow, snuggling in a unique yin-yang configuration on my bed. Their black and gray coats were intertwined, symbolizing the love they felt for each other—a beautiful and innocent embrace of life in its most simple form: connectedness.

Little did I know at the time that the adventure I was about to embark on would have such a profound impact on my life. Our journey is often like that, sneaking up to surprise us with growth and appreciation for how far we have come. And that is precisely what happened that day. Shortly after, contemplating the importance of connectedness and the image of my two cats in my mind, I drove to the trailhead of my favorite hiking spot—a hidden gem just a mile away from my home. As I arrived at the top of the hill, a sense of immense peace and satisfaction washed over me, knowing that I was exactly where I wanted to be.

Embracing the emotions of contentment and being grounded in this beautiful place, a smile spread across my face as if the universe itself was watching. With anticipation, I picked up my pace and passed through the gate of the trail entrance. What is remarkable is that every time I have hiked this canyon over the past twenty years, it has felt different—an ever-changing experience that never ceases to amaze me. Whenever I place my foot on the dirt trail, or the front tire of my bike if I am mountain biking, a thought often crosses my mind: I wish someone was here to share this beautiful day with me. Yet nine times out of ten, I am grateful for the peacefulness and solace of my solo adventures. Stress levels diminish, conversations become unnecessary, and a sense of well-being and mental clarity envelops me.

There was a reason I was undertaking this journey alone that day. Soon enough, I would reach a moment that would literally stop me in my tracks. Immersed within the stunning beauty of the Southern California canyon, not too far from the ocean but nestled in the hills, adorned with flowering cacti against an arid desert backdrop, nature embraced serenity. The subtle swish of peregrine falcons floating overhead, keeping a watchful eye on my progress, accompanied the gentle sound of a babbling brook by my side.

In that very moment, as I skipped down the trail, something compelled me to halt, look backward, and encounter an overwhelming feeling that I needed to capture my thoughts about this experience. I swiftly retrieved my phone from my waist pack, found my note-taking app, and pressed record. An overwhelming urge to speak words I had not even thought of yet swept over me as I continued to walk along the path. At several trail intersections, where I had the option to choose my way, I instinctively knew my destination. It was not merely about the physical path my feet followed that day, but rather where my heart was and how it reflected my life's journey and leadership up until that moment.

Breathing in the fresh air and feeling the warmth of the sun on my skin overwhelmed me with satisfaction. Upon reaching breathtaking vistas, I beheld the Pacific Ocean and Catalina Island in the far distance, close enough to imagine swimming to the island shores. On a cloudless day like that, magnificent views greeted me in every direction. Yet the insight was far more potent. It was the words flowing from my mind, waiting to be spoken aloud, that would form the foundation of this book.

This journey served as a reflection and realization of the paths we choose and how we navigate our leadership roles and our lives. Leading others with love and kindness has been my natural human instinct, although it does not mean I was that way one hundred percent of the time. Mostly, there have been moments when my heart soared while engaging with an employee or colleague, taking the time to truly see and understand them as unique individuals, and listening to their stories and perspectives.

I certainly do not claim perfection. Through my vulnerability, you will read about the speed bumps and slippery slopes I have encountered, the realizations made in hindsight. But you will also encounter authentic personal moments of the success I have achieved, the leaders I have helped develop, and the cascading effect they have had on others.

When we uplift others to be their best selves in the workplace, they, in turn, create a ripple effect of kind and caring leaders. Success resides within each of us. Through acts of love, kindness, compassion, and understanding, by truly seeing and hearing the people I was chosen to lead, my encounters as a leader for over forty years will hopefully resonate with your own inner leader and inspire your choices.

Leadership often comes instinctively. It requires self-awareness and understanding of how we show up for our organization, employees, colleagues, customers, partners, and future. Love and kindness leadership encapsulates my perspective on how we impact others. It takes into consideration the decades of experience and the thousands of people I have touched in my various roles. Changing the course of people's lives holds far greater importance to me than the positions I have held or the money I have made.

As I reflect on the power of loving kindness and connectedness in the journey I am on, I realize that it might take you slightly out of your comfort zone. However, understand that this is precisely where you are meant to be.

For years, I have been curious about the decisions I made while navigating through life and how I have led others. Why was I chosen to guide others, knowing now the tremendous impact a leader can have on another person's trajectory? Did I choose this path? The answer is an unequivocal yes. Leading with authenticity has always felt natural to me, and in those moments, it lifted the spirits of others as well as my own.

I achieved the desired results in my roles and so much more. While the companies thrived and the employees flourished, those I guided left an indelible impression on me. Over four decades later, I find myself contemplating the profound impact based on my ongoing leadership practices and the revelations gained from this pivotal hike.

Multiple Paths of Possibility

"On any given day, we make countless decisions, some of which we may not even be conscious of. However, the decisions we are keenly aware of help us meet others where they need to be met the most."
—Traycee Mayer

As I continued down the meandering trail, an odd occurrence took place—I found myself speaking into my phone, an act that seemed out of place amidst the solitude of nature. Yet the words that emerged were powerful, originating from a deep place of trust and belief. At that moment, I did not expect anything to come from these thoughts, nor did I consider whether they would be anything more than momentarily profound ideas captured in a recording and another beautiful moment in my canyon.

Little did I know that this hike marked the beginning of a new chapter in my life, one that I wholeheartedly embrace today. It is an attitude that prompts me to pause and contemplate every interaction I have. I believe that paying attention to each human interaction, right from its inception, has a positive impact and enables me to be true to myself while showing up authentically for the people in front of me. On any given day, we make countless decisions, some of which we may not even be conscious of. However, the decisions we are keenly aware of help us meet others where they need to be met the most. Here are the notes I recorded that day:

~~~~~~

The narrow path

The path less traveled

New and mysterious paths

A path with many intersections

Paths we embark on that have no end in sight

Paths that descend quickly, those that are risky and straight uphill

Paths filled with beauty and darkness, both frightening and enticing

Slippery paths
~~~~~~

Messy paths filled with confusion

The path less taken

Paths smoother now than back then...

Paths obstructed, guarded by gates and locks meant to keep you out

Paths out of reach to others, serene and wonderfully quiet, some with welcome distractions like a babbling brook

Paths where you encounter fellow travelers, paths with surprises if you stop and look up

Paths where you feel utterly alone yet accompanied by a spiritual guide

Paths that are uneven and cause you to stumble repeatedly

Narrow paths on the edge of a cliff, only ventured by the brave

Paths with nature's messengers to guide you

Reflections of an uncertain journey

In the shade and in bright light

Thought provoking for adults and also for younger generations looking ahead at life or just at today

At fifty-five, I believed that all my significant choices had been made in my youth. Little did I know that the most pivotal choices lay before me today. Life presents us with an array of paths, choices, twists, and turns that lead us to new beginnings and endings, all for our ultimate good, as long as we trust our choices.

~~~~~~~

Multiple paths of possibilities are ever-present, even when we are unaware of them—they surround us. With time and experience, I have learned to pause and consider my options. I often take moments or days to ponder what might not have crossed my mind or what may not be an obvious alternative. Most things are not urgent, and immediate decisions are not always necessary. Yet there are times when we have a limited window and must rely on our instincts, drawing from past experiences and considering how a choice aligns with our goals, direction, or desired outcomes, as well as how it might impact those we lead.

This process can be enjoyable if we allow it to be, and it's important to remind ourselves that options are a blessing, not a burden. As humans, we possess more choices than we realize, often limited by our own thinking and beliefs.

Embracing My True Self

"Embracing one's true self is a profound undertaking, and there is an alignment that occurs when we truly know who we are and consistently show up as our authentic selves, regardless of the circumstances or the people before us." —Traycee Mayer
~~~~~~~

Reflections on that trail in the canyon a few years ago led me to a greater awareness of who I am and how to entirely embrace myself, imperfections and gifts alike. When I am at my best, I experience a clarity that emanates from the core of my heart and mind. In those moments, I coach and inspire others, leading teams to victory and celebrating our successes. I spread hope and kindness, striving to be the change I wish to see in the world. I trust wholeheartedly that all things will work out for my highest purpose, as faith has shown me.

Months later, as I revisited the delightful thoughts that were unveiled on that hike, I realized that none of the paths I might have taken would have been wrong. It became evident that embracing my true self that day allowed me to reflect upon the countless choices I had made throughout my life and leadership. Every choice had propelled me forward, guiding me toward becoming the best version of myself and helping others become their best selves.

Choosing one's path is not a science but an art—a process shaped by experiences and self-awareness. It involves selecting the healthiest, happiest, most joyful, kind, and loving path that enables me to impact those around me. In that moment, I understood that this gift had been bestowed upon me in a unique way. During my teenage years, I pondered the notion of being "in charge" and leading others, recognizing that my kindness and care could significantly impact the lives of fellow human beings. Ultimately, we would all grow together, and in some way, I would fulfill my purpose.

Embracing one's true self is a profound undertaking, and there is an alignment that occurs when we truly know who we are and consistently show up as our authentic selves, regardless of the circumstances or the people before us. That person is who we are meant to be.

Chapter 2

THE INTERSECTION OF CHOICE

Why I Needed to Go Down the Slippery Slope

"Vulnerability is also a part of my story, and I hope that by sharing these aspects, it will resonate with someone who can relate to this unique desire for acceptance in the realm of leadership."
—**Traycee Mayer**

In my early twenties, I yearned for more. More success, more opportunities to shine, and more people to impact. There were numerous leaders I admired, whose memories still hold a place in my mind and influenced the paths I would choose. In retrospect, the choices were ultimately up to me, although I do recall looking up to certain individuals, aspiring to emulate them and make them proud. Their names flood back to me as I embark on the journey of writing this manuscript, although some may have faded from memory. Perhaps it was all meant to be, guided by forces beyond my understanding, and serving as lessons I needed to learn.

I am immensely grateful for everyone who crossed my path and shared the messages I needed to hear—their communications carried significance for me. This holds true for everyone; we have messages for one another, and if we are open, we can receive them. The remarkable part of this story is that when we utilize these messages to grow, find our way, and guide others, something extraordinary happens. I often liken life to a video game, where both animals and humans we encounter have valuable insights to share, provided we pause and listen.

Reflecting on this particular time in my life and why I titled this story "the slippery slope," several realizations come to mind. I am grateful for the experiences that caused me to slip, stumble, and even fall to places that felt like rock bottoms or led me along scary and treacherous paths. While I may not have perceived them as such when I was in the midst of those situations or during the healing process that followed, hindsight revealed their value. It often takes months or even years to fully appreciate the lessons, but with time, I have come to see the worth in those challenging moments. They shaped me into the person I am today.

Vulnerability is also a part of my story, and I hope that by sharing these aspects, it will resonate with someone who can relate to this unique desire for acceptance in the realm of leadership. Others may not find themselves in these stories, but they may encounter someone similar on their teams. Whatever meaning it holds for you, this is my life, and I continue to carry this message.

As I ascended the ranks of leadership at a relatively early age, one of my goals was to be able to have a double scotch on the rocks at lunch, not merely to mimic my mentors but to earn my place among the executives. There was a certain mystique surrounding the lunch gatherings, where important business decisions were discussed over cocktails.

As I continued my climb up the corporate ladder, there was a yearning to be accepted by the other leaders in the C-suite. I admired a boss who knew how to drink well, seeing them as the epitome of class and style. The alcohol did not seem to faze them, at least not in a noticeable way. From my perspective, I saw the rewards of membership in the upper echelons—a fashionable and expensive suit, a friendly smile, an influential opinion, and experiences others were eager to learn about.

At the time, I was younger than the group I admired. I graduated high school with honors, entered university at seventeen, and was quickly hired by a marketing company. I could hold my own among the in-crowd long before completing a business degree. When the glamorous world of hospitality in full-service hotels beckoned, I was drawn to its magical allure and intrigue. Shows like *HOTEL* had aired several years prior, portraying hotel general managers with elegance. Additionally, my prior experience as a fashion consultant for a top women's career ready-to-wear chain allowed me to build a sophisticated business wardrobe at an early age.

Before long, I found myself at that table with the esteemed individuals. Days and years flew by filled with fun and excitement, and I felt like I was at the top of my game. However, one day, I crossed an invisible line, where entertainment, networking, and business meetings always revolved around cocktails. I realized something needed to change—it was me who needed to change.

While those times were enjoyable and seemed normal when everyone around me was partaking, the fun eventually waned, and a kind of nightmare unfolded. That was my experience, and I am incredibly grateful that I met the right people who understood the harmful and even deadly nature of this mistaken rite of passage.

I am one of the fortunate individuals who experienced a transformation and made a conscious decision to choose a healthier lifestyle—physically, mentally, and spiritually. In early 2023, I celebrated fifteen years of living a sober life. Over time, I have come to realize that clarity comes more readily now, and the choices I make about which path to take are more beneficial for my well-being. I have since met other sober executives, and fortunately, most of us do not concern ourselves with what others think of our choices. We hold no judgment toward theirs either. Not everyone develops the same allergy.

Accepting Your Choices

At this significant juncture in my life, as I survey the myriad of choices and paths available, I must make decisions on how to move forward. I am proud of myself for selecting this path, and I want others who read these stories to feel proud of themselves too, recognizing what it says about their determination. Success is achievable when we persevere and understand that it was meant to be. If you need support, I hope you seek out someone who has made a similar change in their life, someone who can guide you through the process you are contemplating.

We can all agree, without listing them all here, that there are countless slippery slopes that can cause trouble in our personal lives and at work. These slopes transcend categories, as they should, because as humans, there are many opportunities for growth. Whatever daily challenges we face, they may or may not affect our entire lives, but they will impact the people around us, shaping who we are on the inside. I am grateful that I made the choice to improve my own path on this particular slippery slope.

Accepting our choices is a process that comes with age, experience, and sometimes even ignorance. It can be realized through conscious effort. What I have learned over the years is that once a choice is made, there is no going back. We must look forward, embrace that decision, and trust that we may not fully understand its future repercussions.

I am often heard telling my friends "Move on, dot com," a playful phrase in line with the tech world we now inhabit. It means pressing enter on a decision and moving forward with life. The greatest part is that we eventually realize how those choices, which may have seemed difficult at the time, were ultimately the best ones we could have made. In either event, we learn from them and, hopefully, have the opportunity to teach others.

Recently, someone asked me whether we can avoid making mistakes by listening to others who have been in similar situations.

I responded with conviction, "Yes, that is absolutely true!" The idea that we must personally experience every mistake in order to learn hard lessons is flawed.

Pay attention to the people around you—they may bring warnings about slippery slopes, rabbit holes, pitfalls, or treacherous paths. They might say "Let me tell you about the time when I made a choice that seemed like it would end my life. If I could do it all over again, I might do this..." If we heed their advice, see their outcomes, and recognize the similarities in our own lives, we may be fortunate enough to avoid those unfavorable paths. While we each have our individual lives to live, we can learn from one another.

Letting Go of the Feeling of Regret

I spent many years looking backward instead of forward, longing to revisit things that did not turn out well. This led me to believe that I had made the wrong choices, filling me with guilt—sometimes at once, other times weeks or months later. Living in that mindset is challenging because regret not only affects oneself but also those around us, including friends, family, and the people we lead. When we make a choice and venture down a specific path, we must move forward and trust that there is a reason for taking that route.

It does not mean that everything will be smooth sailing or devoid of challenges, but we will eventually recognize the present focus on our growth and well-being. When we take the contrast of dark and light and use it to our advantage and the benefit of those around us, we can make great strides.

Regret is futile—it wastes time and plunges us into negativity, often leading to added undesirable circumstances. So, let it go. Move on, accept the decisions you have made, and understand that even if you cannot see the immediate benefit or lesson, it will reveal itself in time. Often, I have discovered that the gift is far greater than I could have imagined. Usually, from "bad experiences," riches beyond measure emerge.

One of my significant regrets in adulthood and my career was spending too much time at work and not enough with my family. I am not sure why I felt that there was no alternative, that it was not acceptable to dial back and still get the job done. Perhaps I missed the memo. It is challenging to recall if leaving early and not working weekends would have been permissible. Maybe it was unique to the hotel industry, or perhaps it was just the way things were when you were the boss. Regardless, regret settled in over the years, intensifying the stifling existence worsened by separation, divorce, and other heartbreaking events.

It is remarkable how time can heal wounds, but to let go, you must make a conscious decision to do so. Sometimes it involves journaling, engaging in spiritual reflection, making amends, or committing to do better going forward and, most importantly, forgiving yourself. No one wins if you keep beating yourself up or harboring resentment toward yourself or others entangled in that part of your life. Asking for forgiveness and offering grace to others and ourselves is the key to liberation.

I believe learning to forgive others and acknowledging our shared humanity at home and in the workplace can do wondrous things for the people we lead. We become more authentic leaders, guided by example with humility. By allowing others to make mistakes instead of clinging to regret, we afford each other the mercy to leave the past where it belongs.

One warning is to ensure we learn the lessons we were meant to learn, or else we risk repeating those tricky situations. A friend once said that the universe starts by throwing toothpicks at you when you are heading the wrong way, then progresses to two-by-fours, and eventually railroad ties until you get the message. I am uncertain what will happen after that. Thankfully, I heeded her advice many years ago, and now I pass it on to others too.

Turning Away from the Past

We all have a past. There are moments of which we are proud and others we would rather not recall—moments we prefer to keep private. However, it is often those very experiences we wish to hide that offer us the greatest insights. In those challenging times, embarrassing moments, and seemingly poor choices, we learn that we are here to receive lessons and fulfill a purpose.

The important thing many people overlook is the need to examine these experiences, work through the lessons they hold, and apply them to their lives to avoid repeating the same mistakes. This allows us to navigate our lives more skillfully and make a positive impact in the world moving forward.

As long as we stay in the past, we struggle with our present circumstances, inhibiting the beautiful blessings that await us in the future. Our focus becomes limited, diverting energy and time from others before the lesson's timeliness expires.

Be a sponge, be kind to others within your various circles and relationships and share your experiences and truths. Through one another's experiences, we can exponentially grow and become better versions of ourselves. Learn and then turn away, trusting that the teachings will remain within your memory, ready to guide you when needed. Do not linger in the past; life is generally filled with beauty and amazement, so seize the opportunity to enjoy it.

Chapter 3:

CARVING YOUR PATH

Fear vs. Flow, and Dark vs. Light

"The leadership contradiction is a lack of connection to others, which makes them not want to follow your lead."
—Traycee Mayer

I remember about ten years ago when my son and I were standing at the end of our street on top of the hill, looking at the devastation of a fire tearing through the hillsides and homes. We felt sad in that moment and, in so many ways, grateful to be alive. Over the course of several decades, we had to evacuate on four separate occasions. Although each time was pretty scary, this particular time was profoundly alarming.

As we stood on that hill and the sun was setting, we could see across the canyon where the entire hillside was on fire. Houses were on fire, the riverbed was on fire, and a long train was somehow traveling through the middle of it all, which made it eerily frightening. At the same time, just below us, our side of the hill was burning in several places and working its evil way up the hill.

It is in times like this that I reflect on how quickly things can change and how much of an impact a negative situation can have on us. Hopefully, it is where we can be clearheaded enough to make necessary changes as we go forward.

In the case of being prepared for a fire evacuation, which can happen within an hour's notice, I might be more prepared next time. I would try to do things right and have important things in order and know that the people in my life are more important than any papers or pictures or buildings that might be torn down and lost forever. This time in my life was a strong analogy of dark and light and how it resembles the impact we have on the people we are responsible for.

Pondering that story of a terrible fire that we experience in California all too often, I was brought back to thinking of fear versus flow and dark versus light, and I saw similarities connecting me to the idea of the leadership contradiction. There are so many things involved in guiding and nurturing people and their inherent talents in order for them to thrive and succeed. The examples are often subtle, and so obvious when you pay attention to this dichotomy. Offering behaviors of fear instead of flow or dark versus light is our choice. When I take a moment to reflect on individual comments, interactions, support, or lack thereof, leadership tendencies can be put into these two categories.

I believe there is very little gray area when it comes to being a good leader or not. I have made these observations in my interactions both as a boss and as an employee over many years. I recently put on paper some thoughts on what makes a team or person feel fear versus flow. It is likened to what makes an individual feel like they are appreciated so they aim to thrive in their role, or the contrary. Light equates to success, high performance, and satisfaction. Conversely, darkness is similar to not feeling good enough, not feeling part of a team, and not feeling supported or seen. It seems simple, though I want to dig further into a few more examples.

It is extraordinary to think that it is fear and dark circumstances that are too often what I see and hear from others when it comes to adverse performance impact. Retention and an employee's desire to stay with a company and even function at their highest level is also at stake here. Using some of my own experiences, certain words tend to describe these negative energies. The leadership contradiction is a lack of connection to others, which makes them not want to follow your lead.

Often, this is represented by a leader being too commanding, reprimanding, condescending, and pushing people to a place they do not want to go. The leader may feel like the employees are not performing fast enough or good enough in line with their own personal interests. These types of leaders like reminding their employees of who is in charge by talking down to their teams to show their perceived power, separating the healthy bond and playfulness and pitting them against one another.

This negative and dark behavior leads to a clash, and the leader's own forced control is considered counterproductive. Even so, these leaders claim that it is the tangible way to encourage their staff to improve by trying to "light a fire" under them.

In contrast, words on the opposite side of the spectrum, like support, encouragement, inspiration, guidance, coaching, kindness, listening, and seeing their human resources as the unique individuals they are, are the greatest way to get the best from the team. And yes, love—love in a human way of being concerned with who that person is, leaving their heart intact after offering feedback. Knowing who you are can be the start of a fresh look at effective leadership.

Revealing more about being aware of your authentic self is good. As a leader, if you do not know who you are and how you show up in the world, you will not know how to lead others in a way that lifts them up or guides your team to long-term success. Being able to stand in your true self and give another human being love and kindness will fulfill part of the job you have been tasked with. Often, people need no more than to be supported with positive interactions if you have the right person in the right position.

I am not saying that you could take someone who is not qualified for a specific position and be nice to them, and they are going to do well, as that would be imprudent. What I am saying is that you can take somebody who is well qualified, experienced, and has the natural-born talent to do a job, and you can light their path with appreciation and human kindness and let them go to do magnificent work. You will then see amazing results, and you will have a team that supports the bigger organizational mission and vision. They will work harder, and that is a great reflection on you as a leader. Your company and the employees you have affected in an individual and caring way will thank you for being the one that helped them on their path.

These behaviors are ones we are often taught or have learned by watching others when we were younger. In key roles, we look up to those who sometimes teach us these behaviors to be strong, to be in charge, to manage people, and make them do what we want them to do. On the other hand, I have also experienced amazing leaders in my life who have shown me love and support for who I am, and with the people on my team, we work toward positive momentum. The wonderful outcome of all of this is that these teams perform at an incredibly higher rate of success, leading to financial and professional achievement.

There have been numerous scholars and researchers who have explored the effect of dictator style leadership on corporations. A few you might want to explore more are Kurt Lewin, Douglas McGregor, and Robert House. Lewin explored the impact of different approaches on group dynamics and organizations while McGregor explored contrasting assumptions about employee's motivation and the role of autocratic leadership. House was particularly interested in the idea of path-goal theory and the impact on individual performance through specific autocratic leadership situations. I write in this manuscript of four decades of my own experiences as well as what I have seen in others throughout this time, and I realize for some leaders, official research is pertinent to further understanding.

As I alluded to earlier, my love and kindness have not always shown through, and they were at times clouded by less-than-ideal behavior. It was then that I made the mistake of treating someone poorly, and for that, I am sorry. I have been able to make a living amends in many instances, and sometimes it is in a pay-it-forward format. Sometimes it requires reconnecting with that person to say I did it wrong the first time, as there is not much that humility cannot overcome. It does not always mean the other person is going to accept the new perspective from us if we made a wrong choice previously, but we can start with today. We can begin again with the next person in front of us and have influence one person at a time.

The Trust Factor—Avoiding a Break

"I emphatically caution leaders to be more aware of their own emotions and words before they become weapons against the employees they once cared for."
—Traycee Mayer

Someday, something is going to crush your soul as you meander down your path. It could be a situation, a person, or a moment in time that does not feel so good. Sometimes trust is broken, and it may seem sudden, or it is likely to have been a progression. However, leaders who are not self-aware of how they influence or affect others will often have a change of attitude that results in a sudden, painful break. The shift in communication style is indicative of the change in attitude from the boss and often feels very hurtful. To the leader, the lack of self-awareness and their own impact makes this shift even more confusing to the employee.

At the same time, a self-focused boss may think the change in attitude by them as the one in charge is called for and helpful. This is a common theme represented by an unthinking reaction to the perception of a loss of power by someone in authority—someone in a leadership role who suddenly feels that something they have not achieved or may not get is because of someone else. Due to the person in this role not having adequate self-awareness, training, or experience, it causes this automatic reaction that someone else needs to feel pain and take responsibility for the sudden disturbance. Unfortunately, it does not always work out the way they see it. Human beings are not creatures that can be punished or like small children who could be sent to timeout in the workplace.

They are adults who have responsibilities, past successes, growth, education, families, and most do not take too kindly anymore to intimidating and punitive behavior from a boss. The leadership contradiction kicks in, and instantly, a boss that you thought you liked and with whom you had effective communication suddenly behaves in a way that appears to come out of nowhere and is hurtful, shocking, and inflammatory. The blame game starts with their belief that you are not doing enough for them.

Therefore, instead of talking like a respected person with whom you have worked for many years, the immature leader strikes out and believes the result they're going to get is that the employee will buck up, get with the program, and magically glean whatever was missing—even though the work has been hard, diligent, and from the heart. Guess what? The opposite happens. The employee immediately feels resentful, punished, misunderstood, and alone. They no longer feel like the person they report to has their back or their best interests in mind, and the feeling we have as employees and advocates and cheerleaders for a company is wiped off the table in a matter of words.

It is so important that, as a leader, we understand the effect we have on an employee. The leaders who lack emotional intelligence and maturity can do great damage to companies. The employee may go away, or they may quietly do more work or less work and go into survival mode. It is a feeling of protecting oneself not from the fear of losing a job or a boss that no longer seems to like you as a person but a real concern for being mistreated in a way that no one deserves.

I emphatically caution leaders to be more aware of their own emotions and words before they become weapons against the employees they once cared for. These contradictory leaders will not achieve what they set out to do but will alienate and subvert their power, or perceived power, and cause the employee to think hard about whether they care to work for that boss anymore. And that feeling has increased exponentially as we explore new generations, new situations in the office, and individuals becoming more aware of who they are and how they deserve to be treated.

I applaud the employees who stand up for themselves and realize that either being a leader or reporting to a leader who has so little awareness of themselves or experience as a strong leader is consequential. Strong means being capable of delivering information and directing their team without crushing their soul. Those leaders are the real winners. And I celebrate all of them.

Embracing the Unknown

"There comes a time in our careers when the relationships and connectedness we have with our team will matter in a way that we have never thought of before."
—Traycee Mayer

The journey of carving my path by looking forward and looking back was meant to evaluate how far I had come and what I might have learned. Some of the biggest lessons were during the times I used my instinct and intuition to rise up to challenging circumstances often brought on by difficult people and walking through new things. In many instances, those things are relationships with people, customers, bosses, employees, coworkers, and even our own family or friends.

As an example, toxic people in the workplace have shown up throughout my career, and the most important thing is having the insight and experience in navigating the situations born from this dynamic. One must try to give leadership and direction in a firm but kind and respectful way that gets the message across to the misbehaving individual while fortifying the whole team to rise above. These are all things that can be learned if one is willing.

Unfortunately, I have witnessed too many leaders who believe that if they ignore the toxic person, it will all work out. It never does.

I was leading a large sales team when I was in my twenties and knew many of the people in my group had more years of direct experience. However, the gift I was given as the leader was to accomplish the goals the company had set forth for our team and I had also set for myself with the team in front of me. Good, bad, or indifferent, they were the group I was to work with and to encourage the best outcome for all.

The connections I built with them by recognizing their uniqueness always gleaned more success than I had envisioned. I found and amplified the strength of each to maximize the success of this team, which included managing through toxic behaviors coupled with performance. As leaders, we will always have distinctive teams as each person is inherently different.

I remember some difficulties with a specific team when one person happened to be doing better at their goals when good fortune and their talents were used, and everything they touched was gold. What I did not like to see was that person become the "toxic top performer" and make the others on the team feel not good enough. And sometimes that bled through to other departments as well.

My team at the time decided during a group meeting that if a person acted out with their ego, showing an ugly side of themselves, the term "no prima donnas" would be said. It became more of a fun reminder to the members of the team to check themselves and to stay in alignment with the team—to celebrate everyone and lift others up as opposed to letting one person run ragged over the rest.

One bad apple can be that negative person focusing on and celebrating themselves too much. We do not want to get away from celebrating success and rewarding those top performers; however, when they display a dangerous attitude and make others feel bad, then the team is at risk of unraveling. That is when we need to step in, embrace a solution, and be firm in who we are as a leader.

Embracing the unknown is a constant in leadership and is what makes it an exciting and fulfilling path. It does not mean it is easy. I am very well aware that my greatest gifts as a leader are the heart I was born with and the point of view I have honed to positively influence others. Many times over four decades, I have happened upon circumstances that I would have preferred not to have experienced. However, after briefly looking behind me to see if there was someone else to make those tough decisions and lead a team through tough spots, I realized it was me again, and for that, I am grateful.

There comes a time in our careers when the relationships and connectedness we have with our team will matter in a way that we have never thought of before. I was a hotel general manager at the time in the entertainment sector of Southern California, and our market was highly focused on families on holiday traveling from abroad. I remember vividly the morning of September 11, 2001, and preparing to head to work when one of my employees who was already there called me to demand I turn on the television immediately. I stood in front of the large-screen TV in my living room with one phone connected to the silence of my teammate, watching in horror what was unfolding. I could not leave my house because the universe and our hearts were being affected at that very moment.

As soon as there was a split second of coherence, I got in my car and drove to be with my family at work. And by family, I mean my employees, my 180-plus resolute humans. We were there to serve our guests and each other, and I was there to serve all of them, including our owners and franchise. Our hotel business was about to go from one hundred percent occupancy down to below five percent within a forty-eight-hour period. Life as we knew it seemed to stop as the tragedy of the day and the effect on our world peace came to be fully realized.

What I knew then, and what I am profoundly grateful for even as I look back at this many years later, is that the loyalty of my team was the backbone of success that would allow us to weather that tremendous storm. All the various levels of connection, mentorship, partnership, and teamwork led to a commitment between individuals and their fellow employees that our guests in the hotel and the ownership group would be forever grateful for. Our owners, as well as the franchise, were lovely, supportive people and would be counting on us at this time of being tested.

What I remember so clearly is the immediate action and an all-hands-on-deck attitude permeating our crew without even having to ask. I am so proud of that team, and when I think back to the individuals, the departments, and those who became leaders overnight, those were true servant leaders with their response to keep our building safe and our people even safer. It seemed like lots of confusion at the time on the periphery, but deep down in the core of every employee were the hearts and minds that jumped in and intuitively knew what their role was. Sure, there were a few adjustments made later, but we would collectively manage what was in front of us.

It was very much like a ship taking on water and everyone doing what they knew they needed to do to prevent us from sinking. In hindsight, there were millions of ships like this, particularly in our country, though also around the world, which would feel the repercussions of those tragic events on 9/11.

We had an immediate mission, and that was to secure the building and resources. We began to draft drastic cost-cutting measures overnight in order to keep our employees employed and save the bottom line because of the way our buildings were constructed and laid out. We set into immediate action following some stand-up meetings with our key leadership team, which made some decisions to close down the least-needed buildings and spaces. We could all foresee that would be a smart thing to do and a good plan for the future.

Every leader on my team took the initiative to trickle down information to encourage their teams not to feel scared or overwhelmed but to address the immediate needs for all aspects. Our responsibility was to secure the physical, human, and financial assets, including the building, the supplies inventory, and most importantly, the guests and employees. What we were able to do in just a few short days by embracing the unknown was nothing short of miraculous.

However, some of those miracles were planned for as a result of preparedness through practicing teamwork, which had become infused in our daily, weekly, and monthly DNA. There was incredible support across departments, and there was a beautiful sense of responsibility to one another that taught us things I find joyful to reflect on today.

Remembering to Breathe

I cannot recall how many times over the years I had to remind myself to breathe. As busy and forever stressed human beings, it is as though we are wiring ourselves to breathe less often or shallower. We even sometimes catch one another in a state of non-breathing when things are tense or anxious, even though the extent of the subject or trigger might be small. This new human instinct to stop or slow our breathing is just being built in. I am grateful that many years ago someone said to me, "Traycee, remember to breathe." I have since shared that reminder with so many others.

People in my personal life whom I love dearly, including my past employees, find it a nice humanizing message to pass along. It is an insight that helps others have a better day and overcome the many obstacles that pop into their lives through the simple yet profound act of deep breathing.

I recall a number of years ago driving in the opposite direction of where I used to work and over to a new job. This new adventure took me through lots of long side streets and cow pastures and gave me a feeling of being in a completely different country. For some reason, other things going on in my life at the time caused a bit of anxiousness even with these relaxed views on my new path. While I would have preferred to appreciate the peaceful scenery, I often found myself in the stress reflex. It was a blessing that I came across something called "Box Breathing," and since I started practicing that more than a dozen years ago, I have put that in my wellness toolbox.

I have seen so many variations of this breathing technique and have heard people publicly talking about unusual ways of breathing to be healthier and combat normal stress. I think the reason for the conversation is that we are more aware of and accepting today of this human trait we have developed of stopping our breath when anxious, afraid, worried, or nervous.

One of the breathing techniques I enjoy most is visualizing the box. Starting at the bottom and inhaling to a count between four and eight, then getting to the top of that box holding your breath for another count of four to eight, then exhaling to another count of the same and starting all over again to repeat three times. The amazing result of this, as many of you will know, is that your breath becomes more regulated. Your heart beats slower, you feel more grounded, and happiness ensues.

All can feel well in the world in those moments and from our simplest task of breathing normally. Breathing kicks in endorphins and gives life to the blood that runs through our body and gives space in our hearts and minds for whatever is next. I cannot stress enough that, as human beings, these little practices are what prepare us to arrive at our destination and help us stand up and walk out into such a better place. As a result, we are able to make good decisions and be kind and friendly to others and to ourselves. Take a moment and try it. I think about breathing being so underrated as I laugh aloud.

Sometimes we have things that need to be done that we do not think twice about. We just jump in because it is important to our own success, as well as others' success. There were a number of scenarios over the years in hospitality wherein a complete transformation of the ballroom or convention space or one hundred percent of the guestrooms would cause a high alert. The idea of turning the event space or many hundreds of rooms caused exhilaration on one hand and a mountain of concern on the other. Sometimes a twenty-four-hour shift seemed daunting, but when I reflect back on my role as the senior leader, they were some of the most precious times. Regardless of how many years ago they were, I think of laughter, I think of giggling and smiles, and I think of teamwork at its best.

On one occasion, we had a large venue space that had just concluded a well-known testing certification for hundreds of folks needing a highly technical environment, and the next day, it was a completely different carpeted cozy ambiance. We only had a few hours in the middle of the night to make this happen. There was joy in showing up in jeans and a T-shirt and my hair in a ponytail to be there with the team and our employees from every department. We were all in this together, and this is one of a myriad of great memories from many years in the hotel, venue, and facility service businesses.

In the beginning, I remember standing in a circle with tired and smiling faces that were anxious to be part of the success of what we were about to embark on. And I remember saying, "Be careful, have fun, and remember to breathe! We may have limited time, but with this team, we are going to get this done." Then, we all put our hands in the middle of the circle with a cheer, and off we went into groups we designed to make us most successful. That's not to say it was flawless and there were not a few glitches.

Yes, we were dealing with electricity and power cords and the biggest ball of tape I've ever seen in my life. I still have a picture of that, and it makes me laugh. Those simple thoughts of remembering to breathe made me smile. It also made the team smile, and together, we undertook this massive effort, and as the sun rose the next morning, we were set for the next group to arrive. Unbeknownst to them, there were these magical angels that were there all night to make sure our business was successful. All we remembered is that we needed to breathe, care for one another, and do our part. Yes, loving kindness and remembering to breathe surely paid off that night and many others.

Stay Where Your Feet Are

"Do not forget that throughout the day, when things get tough and it seems like your feet are not even underneath you, you can pause and start all over again."
—Traycee Mayer

An amazing way to start the day is with meditation. In so many ways, morning meditation has become a cornerstone of my life. It involves active meditation, including reading positive and affirming, enlightening, and encouraging materials. Some of you who read this may think it's a bit over the top, but it is such a meaningful way for me to begin my day. By getting grounded, reflecting, being positive, and literally looking at where our feet are at the beginning of each new day, we can set ourselves up for our head and heart to be in the best possible place.

I love to say to those around me, "Stay where your feet are," and it is a good reminder to not get too stressed or ahead of our day. Meditating can turn out to be such a significant gift to ourselves in order to stay present and truly feel grounded. I love that saying, and I've shared it with so many people that they often share it back to me, which makes me chuckle. Mostly, I smile because I know that what has helped me so much are things that I like to share.

When someone in my life, whether from a personal or professional relationship, reflects on this with me, I understand that we are all present. Being present is a wonderful way to show up for others. It might mean lighting a candle in the morning to calmly reflect on what's ahead, and still, I know that everything is perfect in my heart and mind as I sit quietly. Yes, life can get messy and complicated, but this is the best prevention for dealing with the hard stuff.

Another way to remember where my feet are was recently taught to me by a good friend and fellow coach. She called it "transmuting words." These were all the words and thoughts I had input into my brain that day, which often left me feeling oversaturated around 2 p.m. I am so grateful she shared this new practice with me that I could do instead of sitting and thinking more about all I had mentally ingested.

Instead, I jump on my mountain bike and head into the local hills, imagining the words and thoughts in my head flying off me as I ride. I can literally see them being thrown into the air behind me, and a huge smile appears on my face. At that very moment, I feel lighter, more in tune with myself, and I know exactly where my feet are. And when I refer to those thoughts and words later, they are much more organized and sensible. Imagine that? It is easy to do this while hiking or walking too—just get outside and let that stuff go!

Being able to sit, walk, or ride and meditate each day are parts of the positive habits in my life. Regardless of where I am in the world, this has helped me become a more solid human being and know who I am from the inside and how I want to show up in the world. Especially on intense days, I feel better equipped to handle almost anything. At the end of the day, is it not all about living life the best way we know how? Life is supposed to be fun and full of joy and happiness.

Stuff does happen that does not always feel good, so knowing where my feet are and staying there helps. Do not forget that throughout the day, when things get tough and it seems like your feet are not even underneath you, you can pause and start all over again. You get to make the rules in your life, and yes, you are the one in charge of yourself no matter what.

Chapter 4:

LIFE ISN'T FAIR

Being Seen for Who You Are

*"Our fundamental purpose as leaders is to support that person—
the whole person, not just the parts that match the job description."*
—Traycee Mayer

Unapologetically, I believe that people should not be treated fairly. They should, however, be treated as the unique individuals they are in order to thrive and succeed. This belief resonates with me from more than thirty years ago when my boss, who was the top executive of our company, told me to pay attention to treating people fairly. It was a blanket statement presented without any context, based on some recent personnel event that occurred in another location. We briefly discussed why I felt that focusing on fairness is diminishing and falls short of what we owe to the people we lead. It is also what helps us become better leaders and empower individuals to be their best selves.

When I talk about not being fair, I mean not treating everybody the same because nobody is the same. While there may be job requirements and human resource policies regarding diversity and inclusivity that need to be monitored and supported, experienced leaders who talk about fairness or treating everyone uniformly can make mistakes, as the following narrative illustrates.

It is similar to when one or two employees in a group misbehave or fail to meet expectations. Perhaps they are not acting in the best interest of the business, and the boss calls a meeting and reprimands the entire team. In their mind, this is fairness in action—telling everybody how poorly they are doing and how much trouble they are in. And what happens? The high-performing individuals, those of us with our hearts, jobs, high performance, integrity, and ethics in the right place, are deflated and saddened. We feel bad knowing we were not the ones misbehaving, yet we were reprimanded alongside them for the sake of fairness.

I call that nonsense, and I have been saying it for years. If you talk to the people I have led, they will tell you the same thing. When one person is struggling with their performance, attitude, or behavior, I hope supervisors, managers, and especially leaders have the courage to address that person directly.

To your team, treating people fairly means treating each person as the outstanding individual they are and not tearing them down by including them in a negative energy tirade. This leadership behavior breaks down the morale of high performers, damages positive attitudes, and undermines the sense of support among team members.

I highly recommend treating people distinctly, not fairly, and I have witnessed incredible growth and progress by recognizing people for who they are. I myself have flourished when my bosses and mentors have seen me for who I am and appreciated the uniqueness I bring to the table. That is where true success lies. Connecting with the individuality of your employees is often nurtured and discovered through regular one-on-one time together.

One-on-one time dedicated to our employees, whether they are entry-level or senior leaders reporting to a C-suite executive, should be uninterrupted, private, and include active listening with occasional feedback. It is a time dedicated to the employee in the supervised role, providing them with the opportunity to be seen, heard, and valued for who they are. This is a primary responsibility of leaders in developing and retaining talented team members.

During these meetings, the focus should be on the person being supervised, allowing them to express themselves and being attentive to what they are not saying. Understanding why and how they are there holds important meaning to them and recognizing that their perspective is different from anyone else's is crucial. Sometimes these distinctions are subtle and unique, while other times you may find similarities among their coworkers. As leaders, we owe them the opportunity to be who they are. I often talk about not treating people fairly, and that may irritate some because there has been a push for fairness.

However, there are two distinct kinds of fairness. If we are talking about fairness in terms of everyone receiving the same respect, opportunities, pay, or consideration, I agree 100 percent.

When I talk about not treating people fairly, I unequivocally mean not treating them equally in a way that overlooks the uniqueness they bring to the workplace and the world. As leaders, we have the ability to offer love and kindness, or we can clip their wings and prevent them from soaring.

This may sound like an analogy, and it is exactly that. Nothing makes me feel better inside than watching an employee rise higher because they feel seen, heard, and supported. They feel empowered to use their gifts and succeed in unique ways that others cannot. It does not mean that you do not have a dozen people with many similar qualities. But there are always rare traits that make individuals exceptional. I attribute a great deal of my success in business to recognizing those sparkling qualities in the people I have guided.

I challenge you today to open your mind and heart and truly see the people in front of you for who they are. Not all one-on-ones need to be in an office with a structured agenda, although that can be helpful. It could simply involve going for a walk. I used to call it a "two o'clock walk." Get outside, get some fresh air, walk with coffee, and do most of the listening. That is a beautiful place to start.

Over the years, I have done fun things with my employees, like getting in the car and driving down the street from our office or building to grab a root beer float or taking a little drive to see something interesting while listening. Within reason, there are no limitations to what you can do with the time you give your team in order to get to know them and understand what and who is important to them. I find it exhilarating, and so do my employees, when they have recommended a fun little outing.

Remember, employees are often away from their families for many hours each day. We have the distinct opportunity to show that we care about them and their families and that we understand them as human beings. This often uplifts them, makes them want to work harder and smarter, and fills them with enthusiasm to create success for themselves and their company.

More than anything, it makes them want to stay. Retention is a significant issue these days, and we have all heard about "quiet quitting" and people not wanting to work for a particular boss or company. It is true that people leave bad bosses and bad cultures because they do not feel seen and do not feel important to the overall contribution.

This is our crucial role as leaders—to engage with our employees. If we have hired great employees, we have invested money and time in them, and we need to set them up for continued success and retention. Our fundamental purpose as leaders is to support that person—the whole person, not just the parts that match the job description. You need to think beyond the normal criteria and genuinely see the person in front of you.

Recognizing the Uniqueness of All

"This is the great part of being a leader—encouraging and supporting each individual. It is not just about job descriptions, sales quotas, or company performance scores. It is about taking care of our human assets."
—Traycee Mayer

Around twenty-five years ago, I started doing something called "What about me?" I created a little one-page sheet with little clouds, stars, and message bubbles where I would ask my employees questions like when their favorite holiday was, favorite soft drink or candy bar, what they like to do on a day off, favorite color, and who their best friend or family members are. This gave me a snapshot of who they are as unique individuals. Each of my employees immediately felt important, knowing that it mattered to me to know these details about their preferences. The real fun began when, on any random day, I would surprise them with their favorite soft drink or snack that I kept in my desk. I would also spend an hour on a walk or doing a fun activity with them to remind them of their importance to the success of the entire group.

This is the great part of being a leader—encouraging and supporting each individual. It is not just about job descriptions, sales quotas, or company performance scores. It is about taking care of our human assets. How we make people feel in those small moments matters. As leaders, we need to understand the impact we have on their self-worth and the trajectory of their lives. The way they feel at work often influences their attitudes at home and with their friends and family. People thrive when they feel valued and seen for who they are, and when leaders take the time to lift them up.

Get ready for some impressive results. One of the most beautiful things I have seen is the way dozens of general managers, senior directors, vice presidents, and C-suite executives who have worked for me at some point in the last forty years treat the people they lead and the success they have achieved on their journeys. It is all about them, and I am grateful I got to contribute a few moments or even years to helping them discover the real power of leadership.

These days, I increasingly recognize the uniqueness of random strangers. It brings immense joy to me, especially when I feel intuitively nudged to share from my heart. This applies to fellow travelers I encounter on my daily journeys, whether it's at the grocery store, gas station, walking through my neighborhood, or mountain biking on the local trails.

Recently, after weeks of rain, it felt good to be out in the cool sun with the breeze from the ocean. When I arrived at a nearby trail that had become more popular due to an article in the newspaper about abundant wildflowers, I realized that my sacred canyon had turned into a bit of a tourist attraction. With positive self-talk and the realization that I do not own the canyon, I watched others experience its beauty for the first time. I had the blessing of biking through it for decades, and it was time to share the experience with others, regardless of how they perceived it.

What was fun was becoming a bit of a docent and volunteer historian of the canyon's plants, flowers, and wildlife that day. I shared my love for that place with complete strangers who crossed my path because they are fellow travelers. I took pictures for people, greeted them, and answered questions about my mountain bike. Sometimes, I even provided directions for getting out of the canyon and which way to go next. I answered many inquiries about this path that means so much to me.

Strangers remarked on seeing me ride my bike straight up the hill and, for the first time, had an opportunity to laugh a little when someone asked my age. Yes, I am a grandma and a mountain biker, and a pretty darn good one at that! I am grateful that I connected to my joy again simply by being kind and engaging.

I met some young entrepreneurs and individuals discussing climbing the corporate ladder. It is funny the conversations you get into in the middle of nature. I admired the thoughts of some younger generation members about the importance of spending a Saturday afternoon hiking, biking, and talking with others, and making connections that might never have happened if everyone prioritized housework or career more than anything else.

Setting aside the stress of chores and reports for a moment, we fully let go and shared a common language of living life to its fullest. I am glad I had the chance to meet some new fellow travelers on my path.

Helping Others Thrive and Succeed

"We can be better leaders by leveling up and providing feedback in an authentic and encouraging way that doesn't crush our employees' spirits."
—Traycee Mayer

When I look back on decades of leading teams, I realize one of the most magical moments for me was being of service through training and leading with love and kindness. Instead of hiring external trainers, I dedicated my heart and soul to my team's success and growth. Planning and delivering training sessions filled me with joy. Engaging in numerous "train the trainer" events in my senior roles with a large franchise hotel company allowed me to hone my skills and become an effective trainer. The experience, coupled with my passion for helping others grow, had a significant impact on those I worked with.

Throughout my career, the most enjoyable moments have been when I meet my new employees. I find ways to make them feel special and foster a sense of belonging, fun, and excitement while working toward our common goals. It is important for me as a leader to create an environment where they can leave their job at the end of the day and think, "Wow, I enjoy working here, and now I get to go home to my family."

I had a lot of fun organizing team-building exercises and activities. I would find the right toy or game to encourage teamwork, and I would get excited about the food and table setups. Sometimes we would have a theme related to football season, allowing everyone to wear their favorite jersey. If we were doing physically active games, I would let everyone know they could wear jeans or something comfortable for the day. I made sure that people from different departments did not always sit together so they had the opportunity to meet and get to know each other personally, even when they were busy working in their own areas.

One activity my employees loved was building Lego structures. I would buy kits of complicated sets of buildings or vehicles and place them in the center of the table, wrapped up. The team would choose their own leader, who had to use the instructions without touching the rest of the Legos while the rest of the team followed their direction to build the structure. It was a great analogy for taking turns as a leader and as a follower, and it always resulted in a lot of laughter and passion. The teams worked together to help each other build something amazing, like a space car or a subterranean vehicle. It was always a lot of fun!

Promoting a sense of fun and camaraderie at work through team-building activities has always been a gift for me. It elevates my departments and helps newer leaders reach new levels of impact. These activities encourage people to step outside their comfort zones, revealing who they truly are inside.

For many years, I have used deep and meaningful videos and books from a series called Simple Truths. My favorite book and corresponding video are *The Power of Teamwork Inspired by the Blue Angels* and their training together. The book emphasizes how crucial it is for each team member to contribute to the group's success. This book, written by Scott Beare and Michael McMillan, can be found through SimpleTruths.com. The commitment of the Blue Angels, where there is so much danger if they do not work as a team, resonates deeply.

I have shared these concepts and analogies with the business teams in front of me dozens of times to hundreds of employees at various locations. One of my fondest memories was when I was managing two separate hotels, one in Long Beach and one in Hawaii. I knew I would be flying back and forth as the general manager of both hotels, spending two weeks at each place. This video and its message were crucial for both of my teams, so the power of teamwork became a mantra for us.

To symbolize our commitment, I went to a toy store and bought every jet I could find. Each team member chose a jet to place on their desk next to their computer, reminding them of their crucial role within the team. It was a lot of fun, and almost twenty years later, I still have a couple of those jets. In fact, a few weeks ago, I gave the remaining jets to someone special in my life and retold the story of the power of teamwork. I know they will treasure those jets and someday share the story with their own team.

I find it fascinating to contemplate the leadership contradiction and the choice of leading others in a unique way. Forty years ago, leadership was often associated with being tough and demanding perfection from the people who followed.

I remember a quote from my business management course that described leadership as "managing the coordination and organization of business activities, typically including the production of materials, money, and services, and involving both innovation and marketing." But where were the talented human beings who would make it all a success?

It became clear to me that encouragement, support, and kindness were my favorite words when it came to leadership. The leaders I loved and respected the most were the ones who helped me grow without tearing my heart apart. While no one is perfect, a good leader guides and redirects us when we are on the wrong path.

We can be better leaders by leveling up and providing feedback in an authentic and encouraging way that does not crush our employees' spirits. At one point in my career, an executive vice president told me, "Traycee, you are such a strong leader, kind of like an iron fist with a velvet glove." I often reflect on those words and remember that there is strength in my core, unquestionably paired with kindness that reaches the hearts of those I lead.

I am grateful for those words many years ago and for the leaders in my life who have been both negative examples of leadership and amazing beacons of guidance. Some provided poor examples that taught me what not to do, while others showed me the power of humanity, vulnerability, and authenticity.

The iron fist part of me that was so poignantly pointed out was a reflection on the part of me that is a strong and structured leader. I have coached, counseled, and fired hundreds of employees in my career. I am the leader who also told my direct reports that they needed to submit an agenda the day before our senior directors meeting in order to be added to the meeting discussions and to be sure not to be late for the meeting or they need not attend. Usually, that did mean they should be five minutes early and in their seat.

Most of those employees will agree that I did not waiver on many things, and when it came to quality standards and adherence to important rules such as HR, OSHA, and customer service, I expected only the best. A bit of a perfectionist and over achiever in my own rights, though all for the right reasons. Success for the team, myself, and the company I was representing gleans the greatest achievements from a balance of these dual traits.

This leaves me pondering where that softness comes from—the softness that is not weak but, in fact, the greatest strength one can possess when guiding others. I am happy that this paradox was clear in my journey, and I continue to embrace it and share it with others.

Chapter 5:

THE HEART-CENTERED LEADER

The Humble Leader

Humility is about recognizing that we are smaller than the world but still confident in our individuality. Each of us possesses special qualities that guide our paths and influence others. By keeping ourselves in proper perspective, we create space for others to find their own way. As an executive coach, mentor, and business leader, I find great beauty in holding space for others to discover their true selves. It is a gift not only to them but also to myself.

Helping others develop and find their own light can be life changing. It can alter their career trajectory, evoke tears of relief, gratitude, or tranquility, and lead them to discover suppressed aspects of themselves. Learning to love and accept oneself, flaws and all, is a powerful beginning. We must support and care for others in ways that allow them to be seen, heard, and flourish.

Ultimately, it's all about flourishing and living a joyful, content, and satisfying life while embracing the flow. I call it "smiling from the inside," where happiness radiates outward. It's a warm and comforting feeling of deep satisfaction that cannot be taken away in the present moment. Humility gives us a chance to let our inner light shine and allows others to do the same.

Oxford Dictionary defines humility as a modest or low view of one's own importance. To be humble is to embrace our humanness, authenticity, gratitude, compassion, and self-compassion. It involves allowing ourselves and others to make mistakes and grow through trials and experiences.

I would like to share an interaction from early in my management and leadership career. In my twenties, I had the opportunity to become a general manager after serving as the director of sales and marketing at the same location. I had a passion for hospitality, and managing over 180 employees at my fifth hotel was a place where my heart could soar. While I worked for amazing people, including the ownership, management company, city, and franchise, the most important part was working for the individual employees. I made it a point to know each of them by name and learn a little bit about their families, interests, and preferences.

One of my favorite parts of the day was managing by walking around. I vividly recall my interactions with staff members who spoke Spanish as their first language. Each morning, I would walk each floor, greeting everyone—guests and employees alike. On the guestroom floors, I would encounter housekeepers and their supporting staff. I would stop and say good morning, and they would respond kindly. Often, I would say "Buenos Dias," and they would do the same. Soon, new employees came to trust that my greetings were genuine, and they witnessed my care for them continue to grow.

I remember a particular morning when one of our wonderful room attendants said to me, "Traycee, I don't speak English very well." She looked almost embarrassed. I met her gaze directly, smiled, and said, "That's okay. My Spanish is not particularly good either. How about this? I will speak the best Spanish I can, and you speak the best English you can. Together, we will teach each other and learn without judgment or embarrassment." From that point on, we continued to enjoy and appreciate the love and kindness shared between two colleagues.

I am immensely grateful for everyone I have worked with in hotels and venues over the years. I know for certain I could never meet the needs of all stakeholders without relying on every single person on our team. I treated each of them as the valuable assets and valuable humans they were. Together, we found success.

As senior leaders, practicing humility on a daily basis can sometimes feel less important when the pressure is intense and there are directives, needs, and bottom lines to manage. However, it is crucial to remember that it is all about human connection and how leaders make their teams feel each day. That is where high performance and impactful results stem from, radiating throughout the organization. It is not just about monthly employee sessions; it is about letting them know they matter every single day. There is immense joy in meeting people halfway, understanding where they are at, and finding common ground to achieve greatness together.

Another approach is an intention to send people home at the end of the day with smiles on their faces, feeling happy and fulfilled in their roles and relationships at work. This happiness extends to their families, creating a multiplying effect. They do not feel beaten up, disrespected, ignored, or unseen at work. Instead, they feel valued. They know their work is important, and their uniqueness as human beings is crucial. They are one of a kind, and we are fortunate to have them.

Imagine the incredible feeling of growing up with parents who love their jobs because their boss and the company treat them as if they matter and are special. It is the opposite of complaints about hating their jobs, uncaring attitudes, or feeling underappreciated. As leaders, we bear a significant responsibility in shaping that scenario. Let us make a change today and recognize that our words and actions impact the people we lead.

Seeing the Value in Others

Seeing the value in others brings me genuine joy and a smile from within. I have experienced moments in my personal and professional life where I did not feel seen or appreciated, and those moments held me back from exploring my true potential and pursuing my dreams. We all have inner strengths, but sometimes we fail to recognize and utilize them to propel ourselves to new heights. It is crucial to receive positive affirmations and support throughout our lives, especially during our formative years. Even as we mature, we still need those little boosts to keep growing and flourishing. Life can be challenging, and we often have no idea what struggles others may be facing while we are absorbed in our own pursuits.

A couple of years ago, a friend sent me a card with a small two-inch square of cardboard inside that read "You're awesome" on the front. When I opened it, I discovered a heartfelt message that said, "Your smile makes the world a little brighter." I was deeply touched by this simple gesture and the thoughtful message. Since then, I have made these little cards my signature, buying boxes of them and keeping them in my purse, car, and briefcase. Whenever my intuition nudges me, I give one to someone, whether I know them or not.

One particularly special moment was when I encountered a girl taking orders at a coffee shop drive-thru. She seemed timid, and it appeared that several drivers before me had been frustrated and angry due to the limited-edition syrup being unavailable. Instead of adding to her stress, I looked at her and said, "That's okay. What else can we try?" She made a recommendation, and I agreed to it. When she returned with my drink, I included a thoughtful card titled "you matter" along with a tip. I told her, "Thank you for your great suggestion. Here is a little word of encouragement for you. Have a wonderful day." Her smile was as radiant as the sun. I felt a sense of warmth and happiness within, and she did not need to know who I was or whether we would meet again.

It was a random moment of thoughtfulness, positivity, and uplifting someone's spirit. I experienced a similar exchange with a stressed manager wearing a name tag on another occasion, and once again, the little gesture turned their frown upside down.

During a flight shortly after travel restrictions were lifted, I noticed a sense of weariness among the flight attendants, due to the challenges they had faced during tough times. Despite that, the flight attendant smiled and warmly welcomed me aboard while handing out antiseptic wipes. I paid close attention to her throughout the flight because her energy and dedication to her job were truly admirable. Upon disembarking, I handed her a card that said, "You're wonderful" and expressed my gratitude to her for being herself. I walked away letting her know there was a message inside. It brought me great joy to uplift another human being, even someone I did not know and might never see again. It reminded me of our shared humanity and the importance of fostering connections in a world that often feels disconnected.

These little cards, called "Thoughtfulls," have become a fun adventure for me to share with my friends as well. They light up with excitement whenever they receive one. There is so much we can do for each other with simple gestures of kindness. Let us remember to lift others up today and every day.

Shining a Light on Their Path

"When we light the path for others, we uplift their hearts, souls, and passions."
—Traycee Mayer

Being a heart-centered leader means it is crucial for us to shine a light on the path of others. One of the key components of this is helping others see the best in themselves and embracing the unique gifts they have to offer the world. Sometimes our teams may feel uncertain or lack support, and it is in those moments that we can offer simple acts of kindness and be someone who listens without imposing our own opinions. Hold space for them to express themselves fully. Your role is to listen with an open heart and open eyes, connecting with them to let them know you hear and see them and what they have to say holds value.

Lighting the path for others is about allowing them to be their authentic selves. By actively listening, you can reflect back the important parts and the things that come from their heart. They may even surprise themselves with the insights they gain when someone takes the time to truly listen.

In my coaching sessions over the years, I have experienced those moments of profound insight where I have been able to reflect back to the person in front of me just how amazing they truly are simply because I took the time to listen. I did not focus on what I was going to say next or try to direct their actions because it wasn't about me. My role was to create the time and space for this person to discover their own incredible talents and skills, and to uplift them.

When we light the path for others, we uplift their hearts, souls, and passions. There is no greater team than one that has been given the gift of time, patience, and listening, and where leaders genuinely appreciate and value their members.

Some may consider this approach too simple or dismiss it as cheesy, questioning its connection to the bottom line. However, we must start with a human heart and focus on lighting the path for others in a way that is compassionate and connected. It is about love, not in an abstract or grandiose sense, but in a human and caring way. This approach fosters growth and support, allowing individuals to tap into their best selves.

You will be surprised by the phenomenal results you receive from individuals who have been given the freedom to find their own path and who have been seen and heard. They will not require micromanagement or chastisement for their mistakes. Instead, they will be the best employees because they have been given the space to see their own path, and their motivation to deliver solid results will come from within. Many leaders have made the mistake of imposing their own mandates and negative energy onto their employees when what people truly need is the opposite. Light their unique path and watch them shine!

Lifting Others Up

Being mindful and effectuating resiliency is a great catalyst for experiencing a world that opens up to you. Leadership is about the ability to lead and relate to all types of people, not based on their education, degrees, or geographical location. Human connectedness is where it all began for me and will always be my guiding principle.

These stories are about how others uplifted me, embraced my adventurous spirit, and supported my need for fulfillment outside of work, enabling me to be my best self within work. I express my gratitude to all the fellow travelers in my past work experiences who have been exceptional leaders, and I hope they recognize themselves in these stories.

Several years ago, both my work and family life felt intense, and on the surface, many might have assumed that I had it all. I was single, financially secure from my successful career, and confident that it would sustain me in the future. However, I realized the need to seize an opportunity to replenish the energy I had devoted to others in my life.

One afternoon, I called my boss, who was in a different part of the country, and requested a break in a few weeks to embark on a short-term, adventurous trip. Within hours, I had booked a voyage that took me halfway around the world to Abu Dhabi and then on to Male in the middle of the Indian Ocean. I even made nonrefundable deposits and started contemplating what to pack. I had less than a week to pause my commitments. For fun, I watched YouTube videos highlighting the flight from LAX landing in Abu Dhabi, symbolizing the transition from one phase of my life to another. I was also planning a scuba diving trip in the Maldives on a luxury boat with nineteen perfect strangers.

The excitement, intrigue, and happiness overwhelmed me. The best part was that my boss shared my joy. She understood the effort I had put into my work, and I never had to question her support. She was one of those individuals I witnessed lifting others up. It was an integral part of who she was, and it fostered a loving and supportive team.

Looking back on those moments, all I remember is pure joy—love and humility intertwined. As I prepared my family for my departure, my friends and colleagues would jokingly say "Oh, there she goes again!" For me, immersing myself in a passion was essential for performing at an elevated level. It allowed me to guide myself toward self-compassion and explore different corners of the world, where I would encounter new and interesting individuals along my journey.

Although the journey was long and at times challenging, it brimmed with new experiences. I embarked on this adventure with an open attitude, embracing adventure, embracing a little uncertainty, and embracing personal growth.

The time I spent in the middle of the trip was as meaningful as the time leading up to it. However, the most important moments were the hours and reflections that followed, centered around the human connections I had built. We often say we will stay in touch and plan to meet again. In some ways, I believe we will navigate through memories of smiling faces, laughter, moments of solitude, and shared commonalities. These elements bring us together, not by chance, but by purpose.

I have always been amazed at what we learn from others and what we experience through hearing their stories and listening. Hearing and seeing others are part of my journey in life and being a leader. It was a calling that I had been chosen for. The challenge was keeping clear of my own importance and always allowing the person in front of me to be in the spotlight. Self-awareness, right sizing my ego, and thoughts of servant leadership often came forward.

When I arrived on the boat, I nervously smiled with anticipation. Flying for almost twenty-four hours on three different flights, across countless countries and time zones solo, yet not spiritually alone, changed my life.

There are memorable meetings and conversations with people I met for the first time in places like Fiji, Maldives, Philippines, Mexico, Canada, England, and also here in the US and especially the Hawaiian Islands. It is remarkable that even when we are halfway across the world, with people, old or young, from a diverse array of cultures, we receive infinite gifts from others that may impact us for a day or a lifetime. In most cases, for me, it has an effect on who I am as a person and how I view the world and look to build bridges of understanding.

Writing this chapter is very much like writing a love letter to myself and to every beautiful person I had the privilege of leading and being led by over the last forty-plus years. Even when I was fifteen years old, in my first official job, I managed a small boutique in an affluent area of Orange County, California.

On my walk home from high school, I passed by this beautiful storefront with cool clothes, travel accessories, and some magical things. I went in and met this woman who quickly and intensely trusted me and asked me to run her store and manage the day-to-day operations. I would meet with customers, make sales, order novel items with my own discretion, and set up fashion shows for elite customers to share this little gem of a store.

It is amazing to me when I think back how intuitively I knew how to be a manager and a leader at fifteen years old and how this woman inherently trusted me with her company.

She had multiple responsibilities in the community at large, and that was remarkable for me to watch and admire her connections and drive. It was so much fun for me at my age, and I learned tons of new things. She paid me in clothing at the end of the week, allowing me to pick out whatever I wanted for the hours I worked since I was still a senior in high school. I was only at school half a day, so I had some fun time to spend in the store in the afternoons.

I so enjoyed it, and at one point, I really thought that fashion merchandising, marketing, or potentially design would be the area I would pursue as my career. That quickly evolved into retail management at such a youthful age, managing large retail stores with women's professional fashion.

The most amazing thing was the impact she had on me, lifting me up to see the gifts I could bring, trusting me, and setting me free to do the best I could do. Because I knew she trusted me, counted on me, and loved the person I was, that experience of kindness and love professionally helped encourage me to be that way throughout my entire career. I realized at an early age that being kind and sharing platonic love with those I spent time with would have a positive effect on everyone around me.

Spreading kindness is such a powerful tool, and most of us do not even recognize that it is a huge part of who we are. Today, forty-three years later, I understand that it is who I am. I can reflect back now, as I did a few years ago on that hike where this book started. I treasure the gift of love and kindness and do my absolute best to give it freely on a daily basis. I try not to evaluate who the person in front of me is because, at the end of the day, it does not really matter. Everyone deserves to be treated with love and kindness, to be lifted up. I am not talking about saving everybody from themselves or trying to convince a negative person that there is a much better way to look at things. It is about me being me and you being you.

So the "me" I want to share is the one with a big heart, and although very practical about the world in which we live, I can change my daily experience as well as impact the trajectory of people in my life. It is not only those I lead, although they have the biggest influence due to my role. It is also my colleagues, my clients, my boss, and my senior leadership as an executive businessperson. I had not known until arriving at this stage, two-thirds of my life, that I had had an impact on so many people. I will never know exactly who I have touched, and that is okay. I challenge each of you who reads this to take a day to see how many people you can lift up with small gestures or comments of love and kindness.

So often, we are rushing here and there, occasionally believing that what is on our mind must be the most important thing. When acting as a leader, the most important thing should be what is on your team's minds. Give them the time to talk. I am going to contribute my thoughts on lifting others up in every aspect of my life—one little book at a time. And since I have had the pleasure and the responsibility to lead many others in my career, I choose the path of love and kindness.

Chapter 6:

LOVE IS NOT A FOUR-LETTER WORD

Love is a Human Thing

"Connectedness is like that. You do not even have to know the person to make an impact."
—Traycee Mayer

Using the word "love" in the workplace has somehow become a four-letter word, as in an analogy of something that should not be said or shared. This is sad and has turned our business environment into something other than a form of basic human connectedness.

Love, as well as kindness, is an action word. Both of these feelings and actions are not only a human need but are also needed for long-term success and retention in the workplace. Our ability and role as leaders are to help our employees and team members strive to be their absolute best in the workplace, as well as in their home life. It is interesting how these aspects became so completely separate that we started feeling the need to act differently in one place than the other, and the result was not authentic in either location.

We try to remember who we are and who we are supposed to be when what we need to remember is who we are meant to be. When we came into this world, each of us had a purpose and carried with us many gifts to develop on our own and through our interactions with others.

Love is spelled with four letters, but it is not a four-letter word in the sense that it is considered forbidden, bad, or strictly sexual when used in work settings or with colleagues. Kendra Cherry, the author of the *Everything Psychology Book*, talks about platonic love as a relationship in which two people share a close bond but do not have a sexual relationship. They may even feel love for each other, referred to as platonic love.

This concept originates from the ideas of the ancient philosopher Plato, from whom the term is derived. Plato believed that platonic love could bring people closer to a divine ideal. However, the modern use of "platonic relationship" or "platonic love" is focused on the idea of people being close friends without sexual desire. This term can apply to both opposite-sex and same-sex friendships.

Love is one of the most basic human feelings we have. It is almost like breathing, and yet we constantly minimize showing love toward others, simply because it happens to be a person we work with. Yes, there are people who have taken it too far and have made it more of a sexual thing or abused their power as leaders, incorrectly calling it love. But let us bring it back down to basics.

Love and kindness are the paths I continue to choose increasingly more often.

As I reflect on the knowledge I have gained over half my life of leading others, I strive to be authentic and connect with others in a place where I spend a great deal of my waking hours. I enjoy the people I work with, and it is heartwarming to see them after a month or two and realize the exchanged smiles, genuine hugs, and hear the sentiments of how great it is to see one another. It is not just a handshake, a superficial greeting used when two people first meet. We are now part of each other's world, and hugging someone you appreciate being in your life is a wonderful way to exist on this planet.

I remember a touching moment during a recent pandemic lockdown when the canyon became my solace and comfort. I would see people hiking or mountain biking solo or in pairs, often masked due to the pandemic. There was even a feeling of isolation out on the trails, where we were safer than anywhere else. People were well spaced, moving toward others and then quickly away from them, even outdoors.

The significant thing was that one day while biking the canyon, I found a little rock with a special message written on it. I thought it was placed there by someone kind and caring, knowing that another human would come by and need to read those words. First, my heart, and then my head, had the idea to pick up more rocks I found during my rides. I would clean them at home, write messages of encouragement and hope on them, and then distribute them on the trails a few days later in random places on the path. This is how my "rocks of love" project began.

My soul was filled with joy at the thought of making these rocks for someone who would find them and how they might feel connected to me, even though we had never met. That year, my job was furloughed for a time, like millions of others' jobs, due to a virus that was taking over the world. Despite the underlying shock, I quickly focused on taking care of myself spiritually, mentally, emotionally, and physically. I sought refuge in the nearby canyon, spending the next year hiking, biking, and exploring, finding something new to appreciate each day.

Surprisingly, it felt great to be out in nature, breathing fresh air, stretching my muscles, getting my heart rate up. All that time, I did not dwell on not having a current job to go to, but I felt immense gratitude for being alive and having this space that often felt like my very own.

I heard many people on the news complaining about not being able to go to the gym or missing various things. Meanwhile, I had this little secret of being able to enjoy this space that sometimes felt like it belonged solely to me. I started leaving my love rocks there that afternoon, as if it were guidance from the universe, inspiring me to multiply those messages. So as I continued on my adventure that day, hiking the canyon, I picked up several dozen rocks that would carry the next set of messages.

I must have been beaming with smiles from the inside out as I got in my car and drove back home to carefully wash each rock and lay them out to dry. The excitement of working on this project was indescribable. Some might find it strange to pick up dirty rocks, wash them, and write on them, but I had fun with silver, gold, and sparkly Sharpies, writing messages of hope. A "love you" rock, an "you're amazing" rock, a "hope" rock, a "breathe" rock, and other fun messages that I hoped would inspire others and maybe make them feel a little lighter at the moment they saw those little random reminders.

I put them in my back pack and jumped on my mountain bike so I could explore areas that were the perfect spots to place each one along this five-mile trail. I intuitively knew that as someone was hiking in any direction, they would see these little messages propped up on the side of the trail, waiting for them. I was giddy with excitement and fully realized I would never know who picked up the rocks, but I knew they would be the right person to receive them. I had a joyful day, filled with the act of placing these "rocks of love."

I still remember the feelings of elation, contentment, satisfaction, and pure joy from doing something fun and spontaneous for people I would not even know, many of whom needed that uplifting message. Life can be tough, and when you throw in a pandemic and job loss and other challenges, it can get heavy. My goal that day was to lighten someone's load.

I went back the next day, and as I cruised around, remembering very carefully where I had placed these rocks of love, I noticed an amazing thing. Every single one of them had been picked up by another person. I was exhilarated that I was able to multiply love and positive messages in such an effortless way. I could imagine someone without a face or a name holding one of those rocks—in their hand, maybe in their pocket, maybe sitting on their kitchen table—giving them a little bit of inspiration along their own path.

This became a calendar photograph that I made for my family later that year. I placed pictures of each rock on a month that was special to them, and a photo of all the rocks of love on a plate in my home before I took them out to give them to the universe. I will always remember how I felt connecting with other people I would never even meet. Connectedness is like that. You do not even have to know the person to make an impact. I challenge you to try it today.

Connectedness

"In reality, we all have one thing in common—we were born on a particular day in time, in some part of this world. In the very same way, each one of us came into this world as a brand-new baby with hopes, dreams, and aspirations that would unfold in the years ahead of us in our own psyche and makeup."
—Traycee Mayer

Years ago, I was sitting on the deck of a boat in the middle of the sea. As I peered around my place in the ocean, I saw an endless blue expanse that was the same above and below: limitless skies and bottomless water full of dreams. Thoughts creating energies of expression by every person in this world. The remarkable thing is that we share it. Yes, we do. No matter where we are today, there is another human somewhere, someplace who is contemplating a reflection. We affect each other in life. In leadership, it is much the same way. The better we are connected with who we are, the better we can accept others, encourage them, and allow them to be themselves.

I consider myself lucky to have met so many individuals in my leadership career. I have by far met a lot more people in my job roles than I have in my personal life. Though does it matter where you meet them? I say no. We are all on a journey and meet when and where we do for a reason. Being present wherever you are in the world will always allow you to glean insight if you keep a growth mindset and know that every interaction and person on your path is there for a reason. Look for the opportunities and experiences in the quiet solitude as well as in the conversations and eyes of those you meet.

My thoughts on human connectedness within moments of meeting another person are that we are no longer strangers. We are people who have crossed each other's paths, and we must be grateful that we get to do that. It is the same with others we meet in the course of our work, whatever that may be. As leaders, recognizing the importance of this concept and looking for opportunities to connect can place you at a whole new level of success. As a leader, it is those connections with whom you lead that make you successful—the rest is all a task on a job description.

The issue that managers, supervisors, leaders, and senior executives face with leading others today is not only different personalities, cultures, and experiences, but also different generations of people in our workforce. The expanding identification of gender and nonbinary individuals, generations, education, culture, and language backgrounds cause some to focus on differences when, in reality, we all have one thing in common—we were born on a particular day in time, in some part of this world. In the very same way, each one of us came into this world as a brand-new baby with hopes, dreams, and aspirations that would unfold in the years ahead of us in our own psyche and makeup.

We will show up to others through our parents' first upbringing, culture, religion, or maybe a political or geographical circumstance, but all having in common the exact same humanity as everyone else. How we show up in the world and how we choose to be ourselves and embrace our uniqueness is our own choice, free from everyone else's opinion. Even if it seems almost impossible to make that choice based on rules, assumptions, and hate, we do get to choose our ultimate life situation. This is not always easy and is sometimes an uphill battle with society.

Again, we can all decide how we choose to show up as ourselves and how we choose to accept one another. I am exhilarated when I meet a new person today and I have no idea who they are, what their life story is about, where they have come from, where they're going, or why they're there. I am grateful I have the freedom and choice to be that way. I have the absolute gift of finding out just a tiny touch of who that person is. By approaching with a smile, an inquisitive look, and curiosity about them, I might ask a myriad of things and then listen to receive what is important to them. It reveals a basic tenet of humanity—we are all equal, though unique, and each has a special gift for the world.

I just wish I could spread this message further in the world about the importance of that one word: connectedness. Not being connected to others is the root of so many of our troubles today. We think we are separate and different.

I challenge you to pick the first person in front of you and at least wonder who they are. And if you are brave enough, give them a smile and show interest in finding out more about who they are. No rules, no restrictions. Spend ten minutes legitimately and honestly interested in who they are, and you might find out some amazing things that can help you love that person more than you thought you ever could.

There are very few boundaries between work and home if we choose to live a full life and be blessed by those who cross our path.

Go the Extra Mile for Them

Leading by example is a fantastic way to go the extra mile for those you lead. I would like to share a story about my experience as the general manager of a large convention center. When I joined the team, it was clear that they needed love and connectedness. They needed a leader who would collaborate with them and do whatever was necessary to get the job done.

One memorable project was the daunting task of cleaning out the basements of a building that had accumulated decades' worth of chairs, tables, and equipment. It was a dirty and physically demanding job, but we approached it with a sense of fun and camaraderie. We rolled up our sleeves, put on jeans and T-shirts, and worked together to transform the musty basements into clean, organized spaces. The joy and kindness we shared with each other made the experience truly special.

Being a leader often means stepping forward and showing enthusiasm and focusing on the success of each team member and the collective team. It means not simply giving orders but asking what support they need and taking on tasks that others may not want to do. It means making overwhelming jobs feel more manageable by actively taking part and contributing your time and effort.

Every day presents an opportunity for you to go the extra mile for your team, building both the future of the company and the growth of each individual. They have the choice to stay or move on, and it is important to focus on being the best leader you can be so they can thrive. If our only concern is whether they will leave after we have invested in their training, cared for them, supplied fair compensation, and dedicated our time to their development, then they may indeed choose to leave.

Going the extra mile for them is crucial because they matter, and by doing so, you increase the likelihood of keeping dedicated employees in the long run. Collaborating and supporting one another creates great leaders and cohesive teams.

Chapter 7:

BE KIND TO YOURSELF

Secure Your Own Oxygen Mask

First things first, it is crucial to be in a good place yourself in order to effectively guide others and support clarity. Taking time for yourself each day is both powerful and important. Finding moments of fun and free time is essential. For me, this could be going on a mountain bike ride, taking a hike, or enjoying an afternoon of lunch and shopping alone or with loved ones. Each person's way of rejuvenating may differ whether it is a quiet walk, connecting with nature, or calling a friend to catch up. This is how I often find balance in my own life.

One of my favorite ways to achieve this balance has always been taking a quick overnight trip to Palm Springs, which is conveniently found just an hour or two away from my home. I would book a nice room and make a stop for some outlet shopping before checking in. I carefully choose a day when my business and team are not too demanding, allowing me to fully immerse myself in the experience. There is a particular hotel with an exquisite pool area that I adore.

What makes it special is the love and kindness exuded by Lynnie, the general manager, which resonates throughout the entire team and creates memorable experiences for all guests. Over the years, I have watched her interact with other guests, and it makes my heart smile. She is a notable example of the leaders that impact others. Kudos to her and her team for creating this kind and caring environment that makes me want to return repeatedly.

I affectionately refer to this getaway as my "P.S. I love myself" divine intervention. Even though it is often no more than twenty-four hours, it leaves me feeling rejuvenated as if I had been away for days. The drive, the little traditions I have created along the way, and the people I encounter all contribute to this magnificent time to breathe. It reminds me that as a leader, replenishing myself is the key to supporting and loving others on my team. I am already looking forward to planning my next getaway.

Prioritizing kindness toward ourselves is paramount, although it took me many years to utterly understand its significance. Taking time for self-care is not selfish; in fact, it benefits others as well. When I am balanced and calm, it instills confidence and insight that carries me through the day or week. These moments of refueling and reflecting on the positivity in my life strengthen my resilience for the challenges that lie ahead. By securing my own oxygen mask first, I am better equipped to be myself, lead, and encourage others.

This practice becomes especially clear during significant milestones in my personal and professional life. I enjoy contemplating the places I would like to explore and immersing myself in diverse cultures. I seek experiences that bring me satisfaction, serenity, and feed my curiosity. Scuba diving is one such experience for me.

Since becoming certified more than a dozen years ago, I have discovered that planning my next dive adventure alongside other projects makes everything more exciting. I allow time to prepare and research my next destination, considering who I might travel with or opting for a spontaneous journey that unexpectedly presents itself.

Sometimes, even just sitting in my office and gazing at pictures of my new grandbaby on the wall lifts my spirits and connects me with the goodness in this world. Life can be complex, but when we bring ourselves fully into the present moment, we gain extraordinary perspective. Everything is truly all right in this moment, unless we find ourselves being chased by a tiger or a bear in the forest or facing a life-threatening situation. By being a little selfish and securing our own mask first, we can be of service, offer support, and be present for others.

Take a moment now to create a list in the back of this book of all the things you can do today to be kind to yourself. Spend five minutes making the list, and feel free to add to it later. If you need ideas on activities that ignite your passion, reach out to someone who loves you, as they may have insights into the things that bring you joy and fulfillment.

Love of Self

"By loving ourselves, we remain grounded and can navigate the unpredictable and sometimes chaotic world with authenticity and strength."
—**Traycee Mayer**

It is intriguing to ponder how, despite being taught from a youthful age to love others, we are rarely instructed on how to love ourselves. This realization fascinates me, especially as a mother and grandmother, because I am grateful for the awareness that allows me to encourage those around me, including my family, to prioritize self-love. Many of us grow up learning to do things for the sake of others, often becoming people pleasers in the process. However, it is essential that we prioritize loving ourselves and regularly find new ways to exercise self-love before we can effectively give to others.

I have discovered that quiet moments spent in the presence of a beautiful scented candle in my home, or simply petting one of my rescue cats, can help me quiet my mind and see myself for who I truly am. These moments enable me to love myself authentically. I am fortunate to have people in my life who express their love for me, and I am comfortable reciprocating those feelings to others. When I tell my friends that I love them, they understand that my words are genuine and heartfelt, reflecting my deep gratitude for their presence in my life.

This journey of self-love is a beautiful one, and it is crucial to approach it without an ego. By loving ourselves, we stay grounded and can navigate the unpredictable and sometimes chaotic world with authenticity and strength. Initially, it may feel silly to stand in front of a mirror and say "I love you" to oneself. However, over time, it can become a cherished moment, something to be enjoyed each morning and night. The thought of those moments brings a smile to my face.

Give Yourself Grace

As I write this chapter about giving ourselves grace, I must be completely honest and share the critical thoughts swirling around in my head. It is easy to get caught up in self-judgment, questioning whether I am handling situations, balancing everything, being a good human, and writing a book that people will want to read.

Over the years, I have worked hard to avoid judging others and to love, respect, and be kind to other human beings. However, I often forget to extend the same compassion to myself and can be overly focused and self-critical. But right here and right now, I am going to give myself grace. I am going to step back, stop berating myself, and accept who I am with all my flaws and quirks on a daily basis.

I reflect on moments in the past when I embarked on new experiences like my first scuba dive, rock climbing adventure, or jumping out of an airplane. I did not feel confident or skilled at first, but I learned that as long as I kept going and had fun, I could make incremental adjustments and improvements. I have come a long way since then, becoming an advanced open water scuba diver with added certifications and challenging myself with advanced mountain biking. Soon, I'll have another skydiving adventure with my brave friends, embracing the exhilaration and experiencing life in a way that many others do not.

These moments of self-love and exploration allow me to discover the beauty this world and universe have to offer. So, be open to new things, new people, and new horizons. Maybe even draft a book—just let the journey unfold.

Grace is a powerful force that multiplies when it is given, and in order for me to practice what I preach, I need to also receive grace from within myself. I love the direction this is taking and how the act of putting my thoughts on paper helps me relax, breathe deeply, and realize that I am exactly where I am supposed to be.

Vulnerability is something I embraced when I decided to author this book. I am processing a significant part of my life and thoughts into this leadership book, hoping that it will be of help and service to others. I recognize the impact that others have had on my life, and I choose to remember that if they had not been vulnerable and shared their stories with me, I would not have grown and learned what I needed to learn.

This is my way of paying it forward, even if it means being uncomfortable, questioning myself, or being critical of what I say. I am putting it out there and moving forward, pressing enter, and letting it go. Most importantly, this is written to give myself grace, love, and a hug or two.

Chapter 8

CULTIVATING PERSONAL POWER

Soft Skills Are Not Soft or Weak

"Leading with kindness and love empowers you as a leader, granting you substantial influence and power."
—Traycee Mayer

Choosing a path of love and kindness is not a weakness. In fact, it is a way of using powerful authenticity that enables me to give the best of myself to others. It also encourages the best version of myself to show up, be strong, and be focused on my true goals with passion. This commitment to love and kindness is a profound undertaking.

Now, I understand that at the core of my being, the essence of positivity, light, happiness, eagerness, encouragement, and satisfaction must shine through. This clarity needs to come from my heart and be reflected on the pages of this book so it might inspire you to keep moving forward using more soft skills in your leadership role. Use one interaction and try it in a new way. You will be pleasantly surprised at the new and improved results.

Cultivating personal power is your greatest strength. As I find myself in the midst of this transformative journey, the revelation of contradiction continues to unfold. Some recent experiences are fresh in my mind, and I feel the emotions of sadness, disconnection, and a lack of psychological safety when dealing with certain autocratic leaders.

There are ways in which leaders can behave or interact with their direct subordinates that create sudden disconnections and hinder success. Remember that even those that lead usually have a boss they report to whether it is a board of directors, CEO, or investors.

However, when leaders genuinely listen with the intention of understanding others, and when they prioritize not only the interests of the company but also the personal growth and success of their employees, we can collectively grow in a positive direction. The list of contradictions reemerges, including chastising, belittling, punishments, talking down to or controlling others, micromanaging, threatening, and instilling fear to assert authority.

These actions stand for a commanding approach that confuses issues to keep a sense of control and divides teams. It leads to condescension, mean comments, disrespectful emails, and detrimental behaviors. Unfortunately, this is a cultural norm in the world of leadership, spanning across corporate America, nonprofits, and small businesses. This list is disheartening and counterproductive to our success.

As a leader, it is crucial to rise above negativity and actively engage with the people under your supervision. Instead of avoiding them, be an encourager, motivator, instructor, supporter, coach, and provider of resources and feedback. These actions preserve the other person's dignity and keep their spirit intact. Although these behaviors may be perceived as "soft" in some ways, they yield far greater results. Leading with kindness and love empowers you as a leader, granting you substantial influence and power.

I firmly choose to lead with love and kindness as this embodies the strongest style of leadership.

Leveraging Character Strengths

Someone asked me the other day what I do well and what makes Traycee different and unique. My heartfelt response was that I have the ability to see the value in others and help them see it in themselves. Over the last forty-plus years, I have taken various strengths, character, and personality tests, and the results are steadily aligned. Kindness, spirituality, discernment, love, happiness, belief, perseverance, and decision-making are prominent strengths that continue to appear.

In recent years, I have taken the VIA Institute on Character assessment, and kindness consistently appears as my number one strength. It was during this phase of my life that I genuinely appreciated and embraced the softer side of myself, the aspect that I did not realize was a character trait. It was something that drew others to me, although at times, I may not have emphasized it due to concerns that others might perceive it as a weakness, especially in a leadership role.

A conversation with another strong and positive leader reminded me that our most powerful leverage is when we are centered in that authentic core of ourselves, and the more I have embraced that and encouraged my teams to do so as well, we all perform, thrive, and succeed at a higher level. This is true personally, professionally, and spiritually.

I recall a specific instance where I was leading a group of eight strong-willed executives in director positions. Their qualification for the job was not based on anything other than if they were the right human for the role, having the right experience and attitude to achieve the goals for the business.

It just so happened that the group included mostly women. There were cautionary tales by others, including my bosses, to be careful in leading such a group. However, I found that by embracing my velvet glove approach, along with kindness, love, and appreciation for others, I was able to nurture and support each individual's unique qualities.

It was essential to listen and recognize what they needed, supplying affirmation and encouragement. The energy of my kindness became palpable, and I realized that this strength was indeed a superpower.

Today, I am grateful to wholeheartedly embrace this inner force. Those thoughts were just seeds planted in the past, and now I can reflect on the path of my life, understanding the journey more clearly. Kindness and unconditional love for other human beings are gifts that I proudly claim. There is no need for a specific label other than loving kindness. This chosen path has shaped who I am today, and I am honored to share these insights in this book.

You Be You

Let us talk a bit about the spirit of Aloha and how I was so fortunate to be immersed fully in the that wonderful love and kindness vibe. I took part in the purchase of a historical hotel with a team in Hawaii. There were dozens of obstacles to overcome with the successful conversion of an active business in a key global market.

The property was distinctive to the cultural history of Hawaiian Royalty named for a Queen, and the location on a beautiful island. People cautioned me to be apprehensive because I was not native to the islands, but I approached it the same way I usually do. I believe that if you love and respect the people you work with, even if you have never met them, then everything will turn out best for everyone.

I was excited to be part of the transition as the general manager, a key conduit to the community and staff. Along with our corporate HR executive, I interviewed every employee, getting a wonderful opportunity to know each team member. Since multiple entities were involved, there were many discussions surrounding the care of this team and our commitment to the employees.

After several days, we hired 100 percent of the team, and after a few weeks, escrow closed, and the hotel officially became ours, along with the amazing employees and managers. On that particular day, as part of a revered custom in Hawaii, I was given dozens of beautiful leis to the extent that I could not lower my neck because of all the handmade fragrant and gorgeous flowers that were graciously presented to me that day.

It is also the human nature of beautiful people connecting and coming together at a place where they happen to work and make a living. All that Aloha makes for such an amazing experience for the guests and the team that works there. Yes, the oceans are beautiful, and yes, it is a tropical island, and most people are on vacation. However, at the end of the day, the Hawaiian culture chooses to share Aloha in the grocery store, at the gas station, with their friends and family, which they call ʻohana.

I am grateful for the time I spent working there and making friends, and even in the many years following, I still visit and appreciate lifelong and spirit connecting ʻohana. In my free time on the island, I also began the beautiful experience of scuba diving and getting certified as an advanced open water diver. Diving is very much a part of my life today, and I have traveled to other parts of the world, meeting other people, and discovering more about myself and others. I am looking forward to going again soon. My heart yearns for Aloha in a place that feels like a second home to me.

Traveling on my own and deep diving often with only a dive partner, I have discovered the depths of how unique each human on this planet is. It has helped me embrace the differences in all of us. "You be you" is a saying I love and have often posted on social media with original pictures of my hiking, mountain biking, and scuba diving experiences. I love taking pictures, and I will add to that my thoughts and hashtags, two of my favorites being #youbeyou and #IamI.

What a wonderful feeling to know that we are all individually and beautifully made, and to find that way back to our true selves is so uplifting and encouraging. It takes time and the ability to recognize that each of us is one of a kind, and to accept, encourage, and love ourselves for who we are.

I approve of myself today. That may sound strange to most people and used to sound strange to me. I am the only Traycee in this world, and I am the only one who could author this book and tell this story. Even if there were first thoughts of who might or might not read this, today I know deep in my heart that the masses do not matter so much, but the people whose lives I might positively affect do. Or the one or two leaders who might positively affect someone they lead, or the one or two people who are in my life that through my loving kindness can bring light upon their path.

It is so simple and yet so profound that me being me and loving who I am keeps my center of gravity right under my feet where it needs to be, not in your area or anyone else's.

I had a friend who would respond when I shared about my family or close friends that each of those people has a little white picket fence around their life, and they get to tend to the garden that is within their space. When it comes to deciding whether they are living the right or wrong way, the only choice I have is to pretend to write a letter, walk it over, and put it in their mailbox.

Consequently, their mailbox is hanging on the outside of that white picket fence. So in other words, once again, you are you and I am I, and this is the best place for us to be. Encouraging, approving, and loving begins with myself, and then I can better respect and love others and the choices they get to make for themselves.

After forty-three years of leading others, I am certain there were many times when I was trying to be who I thought someone else wanted me to be. Early on, the company I worked for would have wanted me to be a certain way to fit that role in that job description, sometimes causing me to twist myself into a pretzel to please others. At the end of the day, my best successes and proudest moments are when I am myself, and I support and encourage you to be yourself. We were born to be ourselves and to encourage others with kindness and understanding.

Taking on the responsibility of being a leader is not limited to the knowledge and skills of the industry or company we work for, but in guiding a team to the greatest success. Our greatest gift to our employees is to tap into the best of what is in each person and not tell them what to do or how to do it. We must know how to support each person regularly, listen, and guide one another toward their inherent talents and gifts. To hear what employees are saying when they speak and see what they need to be their best takes a leader with heart.

Not everyone is cut out to be in a certain job or role, and we often get put in the wrong place. Part of our job as a leader from the beginning is to understand who is in our area of impact, do our research, ask the right questions, and know who is in front of us.

I love that more than twenty years ago I was taught the skill of behavioral interviewing and have used it ever since. I am quite certain that my percentage of good hires went up exponentially by being able to figure out how a person would actually be in that role, how they would act in a certain situation, and what behavior they would bring to the table for our project or business.

I also love group interviews where there is a 360-degree question and answer session for this particular candidate because they are going to work with all these people. They are going to be in situations with a group or at a board table where they need to interact and bring their authentic selves forward. Group interviews are a terrific way for us to see if that person is ready to be part of that team that is presumably healthy and supportive.

Unfortunately, there are many dysfunctional teams operational out there, so this will not always work, and surviving an interview in that case is not a good thing. Give grace to others so they can be themselves and remember that who people truly are will come through at some point.

Emotional Power

Emotional power, or emotional intelligence as the word has become more commonly used today, is finally being understood as a key to success when used wisely. I have been intrigued for most of my career by the concept of emotional intelligence and its power in our personal and professional lives.

First, being aware of how you show up in interactions with others in any area of your life and using a pause, reflection, and a more grounded approach will yield improved outcomes. An emotionally strong and intelligent person is able to reflect on themselves and the world around them and communicate effectively. Emotional self-management is one of the strengths that produces a great leader.

Today and throughout my journey, I have learned how important it is to pause and think about how I lead others, how they need to be led for maximum performance ability, and how crucial this awareness is on overall achievement. This is true for retention, attraction of top talent, and financial success of a company in the long and short term.

I strongly believe in the ability to harness emotional power in the workplace, but only if it is used for good. When emotional power is misused, it becomes a sad and hurtful way of managing others. I have coached many people who have struggled with this in their workplaces, and some of them have chosen to leave environments where such power was wielded as a weapon. However, I want to continue to focus on the positive aspects of emotional power because that is what counteracts the leadership contradiction and lacking human connections.

Emotional power, when used in a beautiful and uplifting way, is about knowing who you are and showing up authentically, allowing others on your team to do the same. It is about embracing our true selves and understanding that we each have unique gifts meant to be shared. The key to connecting with others lies on an emotional level. If that connection is lacking, something will not feel quite right, and we may experience missed opportunities, lost relationships, or regrets.

Every person, place, and thing that comes into our life has a reason and a purpose. When we show up emotionally grounded and positively aware, we can have an explosive impact on all we handle. In reference to whether or not a leader who has had contradictory and poor leadership styles, they can turn themselves around, though only if they are willing to change and are open to being coached for their betterment or open to an attitude shift.

Chapter 9:

YOUR AUTHENTIC PATH

Using Your Emotional Intelligence to Succeed

Success is more than positive bottom lines and epic scores on guest service surveys resulting in repeat customers. It has a long-term impact to the financial health of a company, the retention of talented employees, and improved strategies and direction. This fresh path feels divinely guided, and there is an underlying awareness that all is well.

Mindfulness is part of this journey as well and is natural intelligence tapping into my mind-heart relationships. When I am strongly rooted in who I am and what I believe to be abundance, I am more equipped to lead others from the best vantage point. All of my positivity, emotional intelligence, self-awareness, and loving kindness come from my willingness to be in a constant state of growth in all areas of my life.

I love reading about many special people and their growth mindsets that manifest their futures. James Doty is one of those individuals, and in his book *Into the Magic Shop*, we get a glimpse at his transformative experiences.

> At age 12, Doty happens to visit a store called Cactus Rabbit Magic Shop. The shop owner's mother—a woman named Ruth—takes an interest in Doty's plight and offers to teach him a series of meditative practices she promises will help him make his dreams a reality. Doty accepts, and over the next several weeks, Ruth teaches him how to relax his body, clear his mind, respond with compassion to himself and to others, and visualize the future he wants for himself. This last technique is by far the most interesting to Doty, and he largely ignores Ruth's warning about the importance of opening his heart: "You need to open your heart to learn what you want before you use this magic, otherwise if you don't really know what you want and you get what you think you want, you're going to end up getting what you don't want" (99–100).

Later in life, James reflects on the mindfulness and emotional growth he experienced as a young boy and goes on to study Neuroscience at Stanford University.

My own authentic path turned out to be the many twists and turns of life that sometimes seemed like the "wrong" choice and not quite right for me. As I look back on the myriad of options, both big and small, I am left with a feeling of never having looked at things from this perspective before. At age fifty-five, on that poignant hike, I did think I would have made all of the choices I needed to set up my life and be completely aligned with plans for my future self.

Little did I know that this would all unravel perfectly, and hindsight would be clear to me.

Being authentic is harder than it sounds. Much of our soul can and will shine through after a great deal of time of unknowingly suppressing our true selves. There is a lot of fear associated with revealing our innermost thoughts and the "dark" sides that we nervously believe others will judge us for. Do not get me wrong, I have come a long way in feeling that I am who I am, and though far from perfect, I embrace both the good and bad parts of myself. I try not to judge myself any longer and have approached my life just one day at a time. Today, I know for certain all paths led me into being who I was intended to be.

This past decade, I heard the buzzword "fearlessly authentic" as I was drawn to it as a source to pull me forward on my path of revelation. It somehow urged me, if not pushed me forward, to embrace my true self. In these past several years, I concluded that being authentic is not fearless at all, and anyone who talks about being fearless in their authentic plight has overcome that fear that was there at some point.

Being authentic is absolutely plagued with fear and comes with many moments of self-judgment. Thoughts of what others will think of me appear often. The challenge is that "they" are literally everyone in the world we connect with on any level. As a human being, we might be stricken in a moment's thought by one of these judgments, which often arise out of what someone else thinks.

Gratefully, I entered a phase recently that feels a lot more like I truly do not care what others may think and find myself thinking it does not matter as much. Sometimes it is only what I think they may be thinking as reality; they may not be thinking about me at all. It is hilarious as one of my friends often comments it is none of my business anyway what someone else may think. I do not question positive self-talk that shuts down the voices of not being good enough to allow me to be me—it also allows you to be you.

We might all be in a better place in our own heads if we make efforts to relieve ourselves of this. Getting to this place in life feels amazing and a lot less scary. All individuals may receive help from reflection or meditation, as it is crucial to give our hearts and minds the needed space—both physical and psychological.

Many people in my inner circle know I crave and cherish serenity. Quiet time to think comes in many forms for me. I love hiking in the mountains, and even more in the local hills. In Southern California, a day spent wandering to the summit of a 3,200-foot peak might gift me an ocean view, a snow-covered peak, or function as my own superhero adventure. Stunning and breathtaking are my visions that create musings, though internally I am growing and sorting experiences for maximum satisfaction in life.

It is interesting that these 360-degree views are also the way in which I choose to look at life and leadership today with confidence and strength. It is all perspectives that allow for a complete or wide-ranging view of my inner and outer self. At the core of any work or family group, which includes friendships as well, we all take on leadership roles on many levels, and new perspectives and our true selves will appear.

The Explosive Success of Accountability and Productivity

Human desire is part of the core of who we are, and not connecting to others through being ourselves genuinely and allowing others to be authentically themselves is a false representation of two humans meeting. Intersecting with another might be for a moment, for a year, or for a lifetime. There is no way around it, and yet many of us spend a lifetime fitting into a particular role, position, or title we were given, be it in the workplace or on the home front, and this misses the point.

When we are genuine, we work at maximum performance and in the most impactful state we can. A key part of being a leader is being accountable for our team and giving them the freedom to be their absolute best selves. In addition, our employees and team members are unshackled from the constraints of their titles and can be enthusiastic, thriving, and exceptional. All of this energy is created when we allow others to be themselves, and we set them up for tremendous results.

We have tried to mold, squeeze, and twist ourselves into those positions where the description was dictated by who knows who how many years ago. Likely, this is something that developed in culture, religion, or ancient history. It told us who we should be, how we should do it, and when and where. Yet today, I explicitly know that all those restrictions are unnecessary and can no longer bind me into being something I am not. And for many years, and most of my life, I continue to discover who I am—a beautiful human being in progress toward being my best self.

I have heard leaders all around me talk about how being firm and making sure we are quick to criticize and correct the paths and behaviors of employees are the only way to achieve success, enhance the culture, and ensure the sustainability of the company. I have also heard that we need to replace those people right away if that employee is not willing to do what is expected of them. The majority of those times, leaders' expectations are passed down from the way they used to be done.

The textbook manager, aka leader (I use the term loosely), acts in a controlling manner, as if they need to make people perform like circus animals. This style has not worked well in the past for the highest performers and most talented individuals and is even less effective now. We need to discover what works for the people who work for us, and this is where uniqueness comes in. Every person has things that push our buttons, negative triggers that slow us down and sometimes stop us.

Conversely, support and encouragement for people to be themselves lead to high performance, explosive success, and ultimately retention. Forming a true connection with your team, being kind and caring, and watching what happens can bring out the best in them and what they were hired to do, yielding the best results. As an initiative-taker, I drive myself to achieve even more when I have had a leader or colleague who celebrates what I bring to the team and encourages those aspects of me that they see working effortlessly. That is how a fire is lit!

Many subjects drive my passion, and I also see people who choose not to focus on any of that. Bosses forget that someone earning a paycheck is not enough to get others to do their job and grow with the company. There is a dramatic difference in how we connect with human beings as we lead them, and some blame lies in that archaic system of "you got hired, do your job" or leave the company. Even worse is staying with the company and sitting angrily in a chair, doing the bare minimum.

Our true gifts need to be nourished. I love that leadership can be a contradiction, and this seems so clear to me after well over four decades in a handful of roles. I have been a leader and have also been led by others, and I have taken part in teams of every size, from dozens to hundreds and sometimes even thousands of people, all working toward a common goal. And yes, it is still uniquely individual. It is not hard to achieve accountability and productivity if you tap into the power of each person.

In fact, some of my most wonderful memories are when I managed a team of three hundred which ballooned to six hundred for major events. This amazing endeavor at a venue in Southern California was ripe with new opportunities to lift others up, walking around each day and talking to individuals.

Even though I am a huge advocate for name tags, there were days I did not wear one because I did not need the guests to know who I was. Sometimes, the employees I met in various locations, whether they were catering directors, housekeepers, janitorial staff, or electricians, it just did not matter. Their positions did not matter to me, but who they were as human beings did. I seized every opportunity to pick up trash, straighten things up, or make them smile and give them a few moments of face-to-face interaction.

Later, they would tell me about a client or customer in the venue who asked them who I was. The guest had been wondering why I was talking to everybody, tidying up, or picking up cigarette butts, for example. They would smile and respond, "She is our general manager."

Sure, the title is great, and with some titles come many other benefits. However, to me, the greatest gift is connecting with the people I lead. By seeing them, hearing them, and recognizing their uniqueness every day, I saw explosive results.

Sustainable Growth Through Positivity

I sometimes feel like I have a direct connection to the sun. On sunny days, I feel fiercely happy, and it serves as an analogy for being the warmth and vitamin D that people in your life need and appreciate. Some may argue that you cannot lead a multimillion-dollar company, have hundreds of employees, and achieve explosive success by treating people well and radiating incredible positive energy. But I have proven repeatedly that by walking around with a smile on my face and a genuine desire to love others in a platonic and human way, I have exceeded financial goals, amplified achievements, and fostered long-term growth and sustainability.

Ultimately, it all comes down to the inherent value and worth of each individual. Spreading positivity and kindness in the workplace can make a tremendous difference. I have sent and received countless handwritten notes, whether on formal cards or simple sticky notes. Sometimes I send a quick email. It's those personal expressions of appreciation and thoughtfulness that I cherish the most, and I love giving them out and receiving them as well.

Creating a positive environment is now recognized as social intelligence, or positive intelligence. It means being smart enough to harness the power of positive energy, attitudes, and perspectives to guide and lead teams. Sometimes, people do not at once appreciate my positive approach, and I have encountered that recently. But that is okay.

Am I always perfect and positive? No, occasionally problems or circumstances may affect me, but I have learned to turn things around quickly. I am highly self-aware and understand that neither I nor others deserve negativity. For me, positivity is the answer, or what some refer to as positive intelligence—a new perspective that is gaining prominence in leadership. I was born with a smile on my face and a big heart that has experienced hurt and misdirection, but today I reflect on the impact I can have on others.

When I look back at the people whose career journeys I had the privilege to be a part of, I am incredibly proud to see their progress and celebrate their achievements. I have kept connections with many of them, and it brings me joy to witness their growth and success. Hearing about their promotions and new positions, especially when I remember them as young individuals in their teens and twenties, fills me with pride.

We are all here for a purpose, and I am grateful to have some insight into where my own journey is headed in the second half of my life. It is still an adventure, with many paths and forks in the road, and I eagerly embrace the choices that lie ahead. I am fully committed to continuing my journey with enthusiasm.

Chapter 10:

THE THRILL OF TRIUMPH

Be You Leadership

"Life is a journey, and we get what we strive for and seek out."
—Traycee Mayer

Over the last few years, there have been a myriad of shifts and changes in the world at large and also in my own family circle. Everything and everyone came screeching to a halt with the onset of a pandemic, causing leaders, companies, teams, employees, and top performers to question themselves. The epic year we were all having suddenly spun into a void. I consider myself one of those people, and a new and interesting journey unfolded before me with many choices and paths to explore.

Connecting with others and expanding my network through social media became an inspiring experience. One of the blessings that crossed my path was an executive boot camp I was referred

107

to. I met an amazing, kind, and brilliant female CEO who had started this program back in 2008 to pay it forward and give aid to others in transition. It allowed me to meet diverse individuals with various talents, skills, and, most importantly, kindness. Confidence in ourselves and remembering our unique gifts and talents was celebrated. The results unfolded like a beautiful handmade tapestry, where each person I was introduced to knew someone else I needed to meet and added to the artwork of my life.

It was a great exchange of support and help, and the excitement of being myself and genuinely interested in others was exhilarating. Despite the challenges of the times, we all had so much to offer one another, even in a thirty-minute Zoom call. The concept of paying it forward and helping one another became solidified, and gratitude and appreciation grew exponentially over time.

Another significant gift that year was a recommendation to become a certified coach. With several decades of leadership and experience in operations and business development, an amazing female leader heartfully suggested I apply to the Berkeley Executive Coaching Institute for their unique style and prestigious program. Following through, I embarked on an immersive online program that spanned multiple days of intense self-reflection and growth. I built relationships and friendships that I hope will last a lifetime. This journey brought me peace, allowed me to develop a beautiful coaching approach, and expanded my repertoire for developing others.

I am incredibly proud to have gone through this process and spent months on a practicum coaching senior leaders, executives, business owners, entrepreneurs, and individuals from various industries. As a result, a new dream emerged in the form of a new venture, Be You Leadership. It became clear throughout the last few years that embracing myself was something I could teach others to do. Every human being, from the corporate executive boardroom to the impactful nonprofit organizations, and small business start-ups have distinctiveness and value.

There is so much we can learn from others, even in a simple five-minute interaction. Thus, Be You Leadership, Executive Coaching was born out of the brilliant light that illuminated my path and is now shared with many others.

The faculty at Berkeley, along with the hundreds of people I coached, created a beautiful and unfolding experience. A year later, I had the opportunity to meet current students and amazing faculty coaches at the Executive Coaching Institute in Berkeley. It felt like a precious space where a group of humans shared a love for supporting and developing others. We engaged and practiced holding space to gently guide others toward their next decision or adventure. Coincidentally, on one of my visits there, it happened to be my birthday as well as the coach's birthday whom I had met for the first time that day. It felt like the best place to celebrate this new part of my journey, and I will be forever proud of being a Berkeley coach.

What I love most about coaching is the formal structure to support others in recognizing their own special path. It is not about telling them who they are but rather listening and opening my heart and mind to receive their self-perception. Sometimes, individuals do not even realize their own worth until they have the opportunity to freely express themselves in a safe space. As an executive coach, one of the most joyous aspects is receiving that information, packaging it, and delivering it back to the person. Most of the time, they are unaware of the wonderful things they say about themselves, and these reflections are not meant to be haughty or egotistical. They reveal their true selves, and it is beautiful to witness and share it with the person in front of me.

Life is a journey, and we get what we strive for and seek out. I am honored to embark on this next adventure of my lifetime. I am excited and hopeful that my stories will inspire you to pause, reflect, and consider the path you may choose to explore and embrace more of who you are. Enjoy the journey.

Cycle of Leading with Love

"My goal, through sharing my experiences and hope, is to reintroduce love into the world and specifically into the workplace."
—Traycee Mayer

I woke up this morning to a wonderful announcement from a previous employee of mine. He has grown into an amazing position, and I had the privilege of knowing him well when we worked together. I was always amazed at the smile on his face, regardless of the pressures surrounding him, and the words of encouragement and individualized support he offered to each of his team members. As the leader of a large venue, interacting with internal and external teams, I saw the importance of fostering relationships and nurturing a positive work environment.

Today, I am thrilled not only to see his promotion but also the outpouring of support from our former team members who have worked with him over the years. Witnessing the warm response and words of gratitude fills me with joy. I love seeing others succeed and seeing the cycle of leading with love in action. I recall the moments we spent together, talking, laughing, conspiring, and flourishing. It was always about keeping his authentic self at the forefront, allowing him to excel in his chosen field. Our professional relationship has transformed into a friendship, and I am grateful for the opportunity to celebrate his achievements today and watch him spread love and kindness in the world.

For those who may be tired of hearing about love, I invite you to reconsider. If you have made it this far in the book, perhaps there's something to be said about the power of love and the significance of generosity and kindness in our lives. Our world is filled with hate, division, and walls that separate us emotionally and physically. My goal, through sharing my experiences and hope, is to reintroduce love into the world and specifically into the workplace. We all need it, and we all deserve to be seen, heard, and valued for who we are.

I challenge anyone reading this book to take five or ten minutes the next time you interact with one of your employees and stand close enough to see into their eyes and ask them genuinely how they are doing. Then allow them the space to answer without interruption. It may surprise them, and they may not recognize how to respond at first. If there's hesitation or confusion, explain that you genuinely want to improve your ability to care about what is happening in their lives and that you are committed to being a better listener starting now.

After listening attentively and refraining from providing immediate feedback, ensure that you are not preoccupied with formulating your own response. Take the time to digest what they have shared and show your understanding by reflecting their words back to them with empathy and genuine care.

It is common for us to perceive everything as negative or spiraling out of control, but we have the power to change the world, one interaction at a time. I believe it begins with choosing a path of love and kindness.

What is your plan for today? Reflect on your own actions and consider how you can incorporate love and kindness into your leadership approach. Challenge yourself to connect with others, celebrate their achievements, and create an environment where individuals feel seen, heard, and valued. Together, we can make a positive impact on the world and transform our work environments. Let love be the guiding force in your interactions and embrace the cycle of leading with love.

Heartfelt Leader: Celebrating Success

Celebrating success is absolutely pertinent to ensuring exceptional performance from your team! One of my favorite books that I have shared with many new leaders over the years is *Whale Done* by Ken Blanchard. I actually have a copy in my office that Ken signed, given to me twenty years ago when our company went to SeaWorld in San Antonio, Texas, to swim with the Beluga whales after reading the book. I am so proud of the chief executive of our company who brought all of our general managers from across the country together to remind us to celebrate our employees and all of the wins, no matter how big or small.

It is that positive reinforcement of acknowledging when our team is going in the direction that we have worked hard to encourage. At the same time, it does not mean that we shouldn't give feedback that helps employees adjust to better behavior than maybe what they've been expressing, but those "Atta boys" and congratulating the team truly go a long way. I am still connected to several wonderful humans from that company, and for that I am grateful.

Another time I was able to celebrate the success of my team was an epic year we had in sales. This was at a fabulous hotel I managed, and it was one of many in my career. However, this team just knocked it out of the park. It was not just about the numbers and the bottom-line financials, which obviously made the owners and the franchise happy, but it was that momentum they were building with our guests, with each other, and with our long-term success.

I had told the team months before, when we were getting close to having this unbelievable year, that they could choose a special celebration and I would pay all expenses for their team. The cool thing was it really was a group effort, and the excitement built, and of course, they wanted me to come along with them because I like to have fun at work, and truly, it was an extension of how we would all show up at work. Yes, I was not only a great leader but also a very cool boss!

The positivity, the excitement, the exuberance of giving great service to our guests on a daily basis and giving great service to one another was rewarding. Trust me, this kind of feeling sold contracts and made it easier for the team to engage with new clients as our reputation for a wonderful place to stay was out there. It is just building that vibe of total positivity and pure positive energy.

My team decided that if they exceeded their goals by a predetermined amount, we would take a road trip together, and they chose a really neat resort out in the desert. That was a couple of hours' drive from where our hotel was at the time. So guess what? The enthusiasm was through the roof, and of course, the goals were met and then some.

They had fun planning the trip and found a really fun resort with a private casita, a private pool, and all of the team each had their part in crafting this epic reward. We had massages, and we had fabulous dinners. We also had a jeep tour at night through the desert with flashlights looking for scorpions and a stop to look at the millions of stars brightly shining.

I still smile thinking about that time, and I hope the team recalls being on this epic journey celebrating the stars when they were together. We all went in one car, so the excitement of getting there was so much fun, as was every moment if the trip. I can remember dozens of outings I've done with my teams to celebrate their success, and it feels really good inside to remind myself of how impactful that can be. Where is your next trip?

Chapter 11:

RETURN TO THE CANYON

Reflections on the Journey

What a glorious morning in December 2022, two years later, when I had even more reflections on what started as my thoughts on an uncertain journey. As I left my house, I heard the sound of hundreds of birds celebrating, sending me a message that this journey was perfect. No matter the choices I have made, they have all led me to where I am today. I am absolutely exuberant that walking this path once again, I am certain it will look different, feel different, and speak to me with new messages. I am ready to receive them.

It feels like such a huge moment to be all alone, though not really alone. My spirit, which is full of energy and positivity as reflected over the past years, and also in my whole life of fifty-eight years, makes me see even more of the beauty in the world. All those times that I struggled, when I did not know where I was in the world, have all led me to this moment to hear the messages, see the beauty in every choice, and celebrate all that lies ahead of me. What I know for sure is that every single choice I have made along the way has made me the woman I am. They have made me the mother, the daughter, the friend, the leader, and the human I was meant to be.

There was a moment on this special day for many when I was hiking, happily rooted in my core, and aligned with my purpose. The sun was shining, and it felt simply amazing. Looking at the hillsides, they almost looked like velvet from the recent rain, and in the distance, I could hear the laughter of a woman and a man. It seemed to carry through the wind like birds, and it simply made me smile. It was not just the sound but the thought about what was behind the sound that was so enjoyable. The fact that the laughter was audible to me and seemed to be amplified was captivating.

About fifteen minutes later, I actually crossed paths with who I thought were those two individuals. They were smiling and still laughing at whatever was just said between them. After exchanging brief greetings, I stopped. Even though in my head I told myself five minutes before not to say anything, I could not resist and I remarked, "I need to share something with you really quick. I want you to know that I heard your laughter from far away, floating through the canyon, and it made me smile. Thank you for sharing whatever that was with me." The woman put her hand on her heart, and the man smiled and said, "Wow, thank you."

As I continued in the opposite direction of that couple on the trail, I kept smiling for quite some time. I did not introduce myself, and I may never see those two again, but at that moment, we shared something—a connectedness, a sense of joy, a moment of humanity. I believe I gave them a little gift that day in return for what they shared with me, and I hope I will always remember moments like that. I guess I call them spontaneous moments of kindness or random acts of love and humanness—something that we can share with someone that stops them in their tracks. Whatever was in my heart that made me stop and share that with those people, I am grateful because it sure made my day better.

Your Path Has Been Perfect

I am so grateful to be here in this place—this place where all the choices I have made reflect the person I am today. Even some of those choices that once felt confusing and unsettling. At some point after I made them, they were right. And they were perfect for me. The same way that all of your choices are perfect for you. We learn from some of them, and some of them are painful. Some of them are overwhelming, and we might feel like we won't even survive. But we do.

And that thing they say about what doesn't kill you will make you stronger is so incredibly true. In many ways, I feel like every day is another chance at life, to go in the direction of my dreams and hopes, and to do what I was meant to do here.

I am so excited that whatever is remembered on this trip is what is supposed to be in this book. The sun is shining, and this is a momentary culmination of a life well lived. When I say "well lived," it does not necessarily mean that it was easy or pretty; some things may not have been done right. It's likely that it has been messy and calamitous at times, but in the end, it was meant to be. There is only one of me in this world, and there is only one of you too.

There are people on our paths who have messages for us, sometimes in words and sometimes in their own private thoughts. This has been an amazing process of putting my thoughts into words on these pages. While I was actively climbing a mountain and seeing the sun peeking through to shine light on certain areas, I trusted my own journey and the impact I have had and will have on others in my life.

It is important to take time to relax so we can reflect on our own paths and the paths of those around us. I fully believe that unless we understand who we are and are aware of the impact we can have on others, we cannot be the best boss, leader, confidant, or coach that we need to be for them.

I love hiking, mountain biking, scuba diving, and coaching because I get to learn about myself and also guide others. I love that I can hear the cicadas' musical harmony in a nearby bush of my favorite canyon and the sound of a strong wind blowing through the trees. I found myself smiling because a young kid rode by me on his bicycle in his pajamas, with his beautiful golden Labrador bounding behind him. He yelled out for me to have a wonderful day, and my heart burst because it is those moments of human kindness that give to others more than they can ever quantify.

I have been told that when my glass is full, I cannot add any more to it unless I give some of it away, and I agree. That has been my journey in this lifetime, and from this point forward, my desire is to give away as much as I can. I notice quickly that I am always replenished, and then I have more to give. Leadership works the same way as you share love and kindness with the people you work with.

One Foot in Front of the Other

"Choose to blur the lines that separate us by embracing our shared humanity, whether at work, play, or with your family."
—Traycee Mayer

Take a walk, step out, and put one foot in front of the other. With a bit of effort, an open mind, and good intentions of love and kindness in your heart, you can go far. Today, you will encounter people on your path who are unknowingly about to receive a wonderful gift from you—a gift of humanness that is often lacking in our everyday interactions. Choose to blur the lines that separate us by embracing our shared humanity, whether at work, play, or with your family.

We are all unique individuals, yet we are all fundamentally the same as human beings. Enjoy the process, and I assure you, the first engagements with others in this new way will fill your heart in unexpected ways. I passionately believe in the power of how we present ourselves in the world and the profound impact that deeper connections can have. The way we show up can profoundly influence our success in all aspects of life and leadership, regardless of whether we have been in a role for two months or twenty years.

Since my epic hike, so much has happened, and I feel as though I have lived many lifetimes on this continuous journey. Each day brought twists and turns, and I needed to learn from the choices I made. Today, I am grateful for the lessons and the growth that came with each fork in the road. I can genuinely say that I no longer entertain regrets, which keeps my mind open to embrace the next adventure of today and embark on an exciting new series in the story of my leadership and life.

P.S. Remember, the end is only the beginning of the next best thing!